# The Struggle for Education

# The Struggle for Education 1870-1970

A pictorial history of
popular education and the
National Union of Teachers

by Richard Bourne
and Brian MacArthur

Philosophical Library Inc.

Text from 1870 until 1918
Richard Bourne, Education Correspondent, The Guardian

Text from 1918 to 1970
Brian MacArthur, Education Correspondent, The Times

Picture sections from 1870 until 1945
Katherine Wright

Picture sections from 1945 until 1970
Maureen O'Connor

Picture research   Doris Bryen

Design   Harold Bartram

Editor   Max Wilkinson

Copyright 1970 by Philosophical Library, Inc.,
15 East 40th Street, New York 16, N.Y.

Printed in Great Britain for Philosophical Library
by Staples Printers Ltd., Kettering, Northants, England
SBN 8022-2041-X

# The Seven General Secretaries of the NUT

1

2

3

4

5

6

7

1 William Lawson 1870–73

2 T. E. Heller 1873–91

3 Sir James Yoxall 1892–1924

4 Sir Frank Goldstone 1924–31

5 Sir Frederick Mander 1931–47

6 Sir Ronald Gould 1947–70

7 Edward Britton 1970–

5

# The Union's Presidents

1870 J.J. Graves

1871 J. Langton

1872 W. Osborn

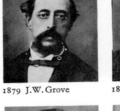

1873 T. Smith

1874 H.J. Moore

1875 J.H. Devonshire

1876 G. Selden

1877 W. Gardner

1878 T.N. Day

1879 J.W. Grove

1880 G.J. Rankilor

1881 J.R. Langler

1882 R. Sykes

1883 C.J. Dawson

1884 R. Greenwood

1885 and 1889 R. Wild

1886 A. Trail

1887 G. Girling

1888 W.J. Pope

1890 H.J. Walker

1891 G. Collins

1892 Sir James Yoxall

1893 C. Bowden

1894 Sir Ernest Gray

1895 T.B. Ellery

1896 Rt. Hon. T.J. Macnamara

1897 C.J. Addiscott

1898 R. Waddington

1899 T. Clancey

1900 M. Jackman

1901 J.F. Blacker

1902 Allen Croft

1903 H. Coward

1904 G. Sharples

1905 T. John

1906 T.P. Sykes

1907 A.R. Pickles

1908 W.A. Nicholls

1909 C.W. Hole

1910 M. Jackman

1911 Miss I. Cleghorn

1912 W.D. Bentliff

1913 A.W. Dakers

1914 and 1915 W.B. Steer

1916 C.W. Crook

1917 Ald T.H.J. Underdown

1918 Miss E.R. Conway

1919 W.P. Folland

1920 Miss J.F. Wood

6

1921 G.H. Powell

1922 W.G. Cove

1923 E.J. Sainsbury

1924 M. Conway

1925 C.T. Wing

1926 F. Barraclough

1927 Sir Frederick Mander

1928 W.W. Hill

1929 C.W. Cowen

1930 Dame Leah Manning

1931 Angus Roberts

1932 A.E. Henshall

1933 H.N. Penlington

1934 H. Humphrey

1935 J.W.H. Brown

1936 Dan Edwards

1937 R.J. Patten

1938 Mrs E.V. Parker

1939 1940 and 1941 G. Chipperfield

1942 W. Griffith

1943 Sir Ronald Gould

1944 G.C.T. Giles

1945 Miss I. Haswell

1946 R. Morley

1947 J.W. Lawton

1948 W.J. Rodda

1949 I. Gwynne Rees

1950 Miss S.C. Bertie

1951 A. Granville Prior

1952 C.A. Roberts

1953 Counc. O. Barnett

1954 F.J. Evans

1955 H.J. Nursey

1956 E.L. Britton

1957 J. Archbold

1958 E.S. Owen

1959 Miss A.F. Cooke

1960 S.W. Exworthy

1961 G.A. Chappell

1962 A.J. England

1963 H. Dawson

1964 Dame Muriel Stewart

1965 E. Homer

1966 O. Whitfield

1967 D.G. Gilbert

1968 Dr W. Emrys Davies

1969 C.B. Johnson

1970 C.W. Elliot

# Through a hundred years

1870
An Act of Parliament created locally elected school boards to build elementary schools.
The National Union of Elementary Teachers was born.

1880
Elementary education was made compulsory for all children.

1888
The Union changed its name to the National Union of Teachers.

1891
The Free Education Act allowed most children to receive a free elementary education.

1899
The minimum school-leaving age was raised to 12.

1902
An Act replaced the boards by local authorities, who were allowed to build secondary schools and training colleges.

1906
All secondary schools supported with public money had to provide a quarter of their places free to scholarship winners.

## Great War 1914–1918

1918
The school leaving age was raised to 14.

1919
The Union combined with the local authorities in the formation of the Burnham Committee to decide on a national salary scale.

1926
The Hadow Report endorsed a transfer age of 11 between the primary and secondary stages and initiated the reorganisation of all-age elementary schools into junior and secondary schools.

1931
A Board of Education report on primary schools encouraged the development of child-centred teaching methods.

## World War Two 1939–1945

1944
The Butler Act raised the school leaving age to 15 and enabled every child to have a free secondary education in grammar, secondary modern or technical schools.

1955
Women teachers achieved equal pay.

1959
The Crowther report suggested improvements in education between 15 and 18.

1963
The Newsom Report urged that more attention should be paid to the less able.
The Robbins Report heralded a tremendous expansion in universities and colleges of education.

1965
LEAs were asked by the government to submit schemes for comprehensive secondary schooling.

1967
The Plowden Report welcomed modern developments in primary teaching and called for a better deal for underprivileged areas.

1969
The Union launched its biggest ever campaign to achieve decent salaries for teachers.

# Introduction

by Sir Ronald Gould

The National Union of Elementary Teachers was established in 1870, though the word 'Elementary' was soon to be dropped from its title. The opposition of the weak, disorganised and fragmented teaching profession to the Revised Codes (that is, Payment by Results) had proved futile, and thus teachers were at last persuaded to join together into a national organisation to make opposition more effective.

In the same year the first really important Education Act reached the Statute Book. Unfortunately, though it marked an advance in thinking at that time in that it ensured a limited education for all, it reflected a now out-moded class-consciousness about education, and embodied a compromise about Church control of education far from acceptable to large numbers of people. Some wanted full church control; some full public control. Yet the Act created a system of dual-control in which 'Board schools' were wholly maintained, and 'non-provided', or church schools, partially maintained by the public, and this compromise solution which was necessary if educational advance was to be made, caused bitter controversy until quite recently.

Robert Lowe, not the most-loved figure by teachers of the day, characterised the situation rather well when he said in his speech on the Third Reading of the 1867 Reform Bill:

'I was opposed to centralisation; I am ready to accept centralisation; I was opposed to an education rate, I am now ready to accept it . . . The question is no longer a religious question, it has become a political one . . . You have placed the government in the hands of the masses, and you must therefore give them education'.

But the realisation that elementary education was an essential basis for a modern industrial state, the agitation against the Revised Codes which involved 'payment by results' and distorted methods and curricula, made reform imperative, despite the opposition of the cost-conscious and some church interests. J. J. Graves, the Union's first President, succinctly expressed the Union's position during those turbulent times in his opening speech to Conference:

'We inaugurate in founding this "National Union of Elementary Teachers" no aggressive association. We desire to assail nobody. We do desire to think and act as reasonable and educated men, to advocate improvements in our educational schemes and machinery, to look after the welfare of the nation as far as elementary education affects it, and at the same time try to advance our own interests, convinced that by the elevation of the teacher, we elevate the value of education, and accelerate the progress of civilisation'.

This general declaration of the 'faith' of the Union was expressed in nine practical aims:

1. Control of entrance to the profession and teachers' registration
2. The recruitment of teachers to the inspectorate
3. The gaining of the right of appeal
4. Superannuation
5. The revision of the educational code
6. The gaining of security of tenure
7. Freedom from compulsory extraneous duties
8. Adequate salaries
9. Freedom from 'obnoxious interference'.

Over the years the Union has achieved in the main all these aims except the first and the eighth, and new aims, inspired by the spirit of J. J. Graves' Presidential Address, have been formulated.

I have stressed this early history of the Union as it is germane to understanding the Union position on all the major issues of the past one hundred years. The nine aims illustrate clearly the Union's determination to view its professional and educational objectives as being of equal import. Ever since, the leadership of the Union has always been totally convinced that their vision of a desirable educational system could not in any way be at variance with the well-being of teachers within that system. For them, there was, and could be, no dichotomy between the interests of education and the interests of the teachers.

At all times during the past 100 years the Union has rightly been ahead of its time. As mentioned earlier, the Union soon dropped 'Elementary' from its name, and accordingly its membership were the first to reject the notions that secondary and elementary teachers and elementary and secondary children differed so much in kind that they needed to be segregated into completely separate organisations. However, it was not until 1944 that the law enacted that all children should receive both primary and secondary education and that the concept that elementary education alone was good enough for the working classes began to wither and die. But, alas, despite the constant advocacy of the NUT, teachers generally have not yet realised the need for professional unity to match the unity of the education service. They are fragmented in separate organisations and enjoy less power than they should, to the distress of the far-sighted, the confusion of the public, and the amazement of teachers from emergent countries.

The Acts of 1870 and 1902, however, created a unified central department of education from three competing departments; and education was grafted into a local government structure that was never designed to support it.

Throughout the period 1902 to 1944 the Union resisted 'the further encroachment of the Churches into school territory'. During the Great Depression that in Britain embraced almost the whole of the '20s and 30s', the Union effectively fought governments, economists and much of the press, in order to keep the educational system intact. There were, however, appalling set-backs: the failure to raise the school leaving age to 15 because the churches claimed that inadequate grants prevented them from reorganising their schools; teacher unemployment, savagely-cut building programmes and a 10 per cent cut in teachers' salaries, which was not fully restored until four years had elapsed.

The success of the Union in its campaign against economic and church interests in the two decades before the Second World War placed the Union in a strong position for the complicated negotiations that were to take place before the 1943 Bill finally reached the Statute Book. Indeed, much of the substance of the Bill had been advocated by the NUT in a booklet published during the preliminary discussion. The Act's great achievement was the introduction of three stages of education, primary, secondary and further (including higher), which had been an ideal near to the heart of the Union for many years. The religious settlement, whilst far from being all that the Union wanted (and, indeed, far from what the churches desired), had one great merit; it enabled education to advance free or largely free from sectarian strife. Never since has it been necessary for me to say, as did my predecessor, Sir Frederick Mander: 'The dual system lies like a tank trap across the highway of educational advance'.

The 1944 Act has proved to be one of the great landmarks in educational legislation. It has been a springboard to educational opportunities unforeseen even when the Act was passed. Free universal secondary education and grant-aided higher and further education has produced a social and geographic mobility that is revolutionising society, socially, politically and economically.

But even this great Act which Mr Butler, the Minister mainly responsible for the Act, described at the time as a synthesis rather than a compromise—

A synthesis between order and liberty, between local initiative and national direction, between the voluntary agencies and the State, between the private life of a school and the public life of the district which it serves, between manual and intellectual skill and between those better and less well endowed,

has now ceased to be a clarion call to education advance.

The teachers were soon to realise that the philosophy of 'age, aptitude and ability', accompanied by selection at 11 and the tripartite system, were really not appropriate to the needs and demands of the nation's children in the new technological society. The comprehensive school is both a product of, and a herald of, a different concept of individuals and of society. The teachers in their new comprehensives, bilaterals and secondary moderns refused to accept the philosophy of tripartism and as a result of their foresight and enthusiasm secondary education developed at such a pace that by 1960 over 30 per cent of the school children taking GCE 'O' level were outside the grammar school system. More than anything else, the confidence and far-sightedness of the innovating teachers of the 50s and 60s, together with heightened pupil and parental aspiration, and the publicising of all this by the NUT and others, have created the demand for a new Act.

On the professional side, the introduction of the basic scale, and eventually the establishment of equal pay for women in 1961, should have created far greater unity in the teaching profession. The continued existence of inadequate salaries, however, connived at and encouraged by the central Government, has resulted in these considerable achievements being unnoticed and unsung.

The main outstanding professional issue, other than salaries, remains a Teachers' General Council; a desire and an aspiration of teachers for over one hundred years. At last another round of negotiations is well under way and with general good will the Teachers' General Council could be established in 1970.

The stage is set for a major new Education Act in the early 1970's. Internal committees of the Union have been as thorough in preparing evidence on the expected new legislation and the reform of the structure of local government as were their predecessors in the early 40s. A major new Education Act will no doubt be placed on the Statute Book, but all the indications are that its birth will be difficult and its early childhood fraught with strife.

Once again, as in 1870, 1902 and 1918, there are forces of privilege and influence in society which would deny further educational advance and would denigrate those who desire such advance. There are many from all walks of life who yearn for yester-year, or, failing that, cling to the *status quo* as the most acceptable alternative. For them superior education for the select few, formal lessons with chalk, talk and books, and children and teachers who 'know their place' is their vision of the New Jerusalem.

There exists, too, another group of false prophets – the economists of the 30s, returned in a new guise as the purveyors of the new religion, cost-benefit analysis. Many (though fortunately not all) know much about price and nothing of value, and advocate policies which would undermine and destroy the character and the essence of the emerging educational system.

What in fact is happening is that our contemporary society is witnessing upheavals similar to those to which this book bears witness. The advent of universal secondary education has produced unexpected changes, just as the advent of universal primary education did years ago. The necessary social, intellectual and economic adjustments are causing controversy. The consequence of universal secondary education is an insistent demand for more and more higher education, the most costly of all forms of education, and unfortunately, here as elsewhere, achievement limps behind aspiration.

These are the challenges that many cannot and will not face. If the last hundred years are any indication, then the Union and its members will once again be advocating a pincer advance on the educational and professional fronts. No doubt once again the Union will be opposed and berated; the insults of the past will be revived; 'a Frankenstein monster which has suddenly grown to full life', or 'an unscrupulous organisation only interested in its own benefits', or 'the illegitimate offspring . . . of the NUT'.

Be that as it may, the Union will continue to act as our predecessors did, adhering firmly to J. J. Graves' century-old declaration of faith, but using to greater effect our increased resources to grapple with new problems and to define new objectives.

*Ronald Gould*

# State education begins and the National Union of Teachers is born

'Our purpose in this Bill is to bring elementary education within the reach of every English home; aye, and within the reach of those children who have no homes.' In these words, W. E. Forster introduced his measure in February 1870. The schooling provided under the Act was neither free nor fully compulsory, and it was aptly named elementary. Still, it was an important step.

In 1870, too, separate teachers' organisations came together to form the National Union of Teachers. During the next 30 years the Union worked to raise their own status and widen the scope of elementary education.

Dudley Heath's drawing of a schoolboy at a Board school, ragged but literate

# Rote learning and Victorian charity

Before 1870, elementary education for working-class children was a patchwork affair provided by private bodies, principally religious. But from 1833 parliament made grants to them and inevitably began to tell them how to spend the money. In 1839, the Committee of Council for Education was created, with Sir James Kay-Shuttleworth as secretary.

It was an inspired appointment. He created the inspectorate, then in 1846 the famous Minutes gave official form to the pupil-teacher system. Intelligent (and moral) elementary pupils were apprenticed as pupil-teachers and the best of them sent to training college, at government expense. As teachers they received an augmentation grant and retiring pension. Teachers began to feel themselves a profession.

But soon taxpayers were complaining about heavy expenditure on education – a recurring theme in the history of education. The 1861 Revised Code which aimed at 'cheap and efficient' education cut direct payments to teachers, reversing the trend towards civil service status. The impetus towards extending elementary education was overwhelming, however, and in 1868 the new Liberal government pledged itself to introduce a Bill.

1. A Church of England school which served the parish of Kingham in Oxfordshire. This building was demolished in 1910.

## The 3 Rs for the lower classes

2.  A Quaker school under John Bunyan's meeting house.

3.  A school in Borough Road in the East End of London run by the British and Foreign School Society, a Nonconformist body. It was directed on the monitorial principle, with a single master teaching very large numbers through senior pupils. The toys seen hanging on the rafters could be won by getting good marks.

4.  George Cruikshank in 1839 reflects the general image of teachers – not without reason, for many were men who had failed at other trades. As their calibre and training improved, they were then criticised for being 'over-educated' and 'aping their betters.'

5.  Quite apart from religious and charitable schools, 'dame' or common schools were operated by the private enterprise of people who were often barely literate.

6.  Only about 40 per cent of the population could read.

1. Since most schools charged fees, the only educational opportunities open to the really poor were 'ragged schools', like this one in Clare Market in 1869. It would have been a brilliant teacher who could give even a smattering of education to these starving children.

**Classics for the upper classes**

2. The schoolroom at Winchester. Local grammar schools still admitted free scholars, but Winchester and the other public schools had become the prerogative of the rich. Conditions were often chaotic and the education rigidly classical. Private academies could be a 'better buy' for the well-to-do.

3. An Eton boy on his first day at college.

# 'You have placed the government in the hands of the masses; you must therefore give them education'

Robert Lowe, as Vice-President of the Committee of Council, had in 1861 succeeded in retarding the growth of elementary education through the Revised Code. But as this quotation from his speech in the debate on Disraeli's 1867 Reform Bill shows, he was quick to appreciate the implications of extending the franchise to the urban working-class. The new voters promptly put the Liberals in power.

5. In Sheffield, the Radical A. J. Mundella replaced the moderate J. A. Roebuck as Liberal candidate. An 'advanced' educationist, Mundella took a leading part in the discussions leading up to the 1870 Act and in 1880 became Vice-President in charge of the Education Department. In the cartoon, the workmen are telling Roebuck that 'Mundella is the man of our choice'.

6. In spite of poor schooling, the desire for literacy was great. Workers from the cotton-mills using the free reading-room in Manchester library. From 1850, local authorities were allowed to finance public libraries.

4. Employers were beginning to realise than an educated work-force was necessary both in factories to operate the sophisticated machinery and in offices as clerks.

4

5

6

# Prejudice and religious faction hold up reform

1. The first half of the 19th century saw the hardening of religious differences between the Church of England, influenced by the Oxford movement, and the Nonconformists. Arguments about religious education delayed the introduction of a bill to reform education.

2. To many it seemed wrong to force children to go to school. Similar attitudes are to be found today among those who oppose the raising of the school leaving age.

3. Joseph Chamberlain, who with A. J. Mundella and Charles Dilke, led the National Education League, one of the two main pressure groups influencing the contents of the Bill.

PUNCH, OR THE LONDON CHARIVARI.—July 2, 1870.

"OBSTRUCTIVES."

Mr. Punch (to Bull A D. "YES, IT'S ALL VERY WELL TO SAY, 'GO TO SCHOOL!' HOW ARE THEY TO GO TO SCHOOL WITH THOSE PEOPLE QUARRELLING IN THE DOORWAY? WHY DON'T YOU MAKE 'EM 'MOVE ON'?"

1

2

3

4 and 5. The Vice-President of the Committee of Council, W. E. Forster, as Spy saw him in 1869; and as a grateful nation commemorated him in a statue on the Victoria Embankment.

6. The National Education League, with a Radical platform of free, unsectarian and compulsory education supported by rates, was opposed by the National Education Union, who wanted to build on the existing denominational system. Lobbying was a more formal affair in those days, as this *Illustrated London News* picture shows. Gladstone and Forster publicly received the Union and the League in turn, as well as many other interested bodies.

4

5

6

# Education on the rates and the dual system

The 1870 Act empowered the Education Department to set up School Boards in areas where there were not enough voluntary schools, with the duty of 'filling the gaps'. The School Boards were allowed to raise a local rate and to insist on compulsory attendance up to 13 if they wished. School fees were not abolished and elementary schools were defined as those with fees up to a maximum of 9d a week. Voluntary schools received a 50 per cent grant from the Education Department but no more building grants.

THE EDUCATION PROBLEM.

Master Forster. "PLEASE, M'M, I'VE DONE IT, M'M!"
Schoolmistress (Britannia). "AND HOW HAVE YOU DONE IT, WILLIAM?"
Master Forster. "PLEASE, M'M, I'VE REDUCED ALL THE FRACTIONS TO THE LOWEST CO DENOMINATION."
Schoolmistress. "GOOD BOY! GO UP!"

1                                    2

1 and 2. Forster's main achievement was to find a compromise settlement for religious education. Pupils were given the right to withdraw from religious instruction, even in voluntary schools. An amendment moved by Cowper-Temple stated that in schools 'hereafter established by means of local rates, no catechism or religious formulary which is distinctive to any particular denomination shall be taught.'

W. E. Forster is the subject of both these cartoons. On the left he is telling the children: 'Well, my little people, we have been gravely and earnestly considering whether you may learn to read. I am happy to tell you that subject to a variety of restrictions, conscience clauses, and the consent of your vestries—YOU MAY!'

3

# The teachers unite

3. Several elementary teachers' organisations, mainly based on denominational groupings, had found a common basis for action over the Bill. In June 1870, at King's College, London, the National Union of Elementary Teachers was founded. 'Elementary' was dropped from the title in 1888, for by that time membership and activities had widened considerably. By 1873 when this picture was taken at the annual conference at Bristol, membership was 6,880.

The Union on the whole approved the terms of the Bill. By training and outlook they were in favour of religious education and welcomed the survival of the voluntary schools. But they feared that the need for more teachers might lead to 'dilution' and, even at this early date, saw the Act as only the first step towards free and universal education from elementary school to university.

# The 1870 Act is passed and the Union is founded

The National Union of Elementary Teachers, founded at a meeting at King's College, London on June 25, 1870, was the product of a defeat. It was born of an awareness by certificated teachers – a small select minority of the teaching force at that time, but recognised by Matthew Arnold and others to be some of the best qualified teachers in Europe – that only by combining the local groups of denominational and other teachers could they exert their due influence on the direction of educational affairs. For in 1861, crashing down on the evolving prestige of the certificated teachers, had come the reactionary, economical, disastrous promulgation of the Revised Code and the system of 'payment by results'. All the other grievances of the teachers in 1870 – that the Government could alter the standard of their certificate at will, that the Government had gone back on its promise of 1846 to set up a pension system, that the views of the professionals had carried little weight in the preparation of the new Education Act of 1870 – can only be understood against an overwhelming feeling of anger and betrayal in the 60s.

What was the condition of the schools, of education and of teachers in the era prior to 1870? This of course was the blooming period of the Victorian age, a period of a largely unreformed franchise which kept the vote from the working classes, of the triumph of ideas of liberal economy, of fearful exploitation and long working hours in industrial areas, of burgeoning confidence in the middle classes, of the 'progressive' notions of Albert, the Prince Consort. All the cross-winds in the most advanced industrial society that the world had yet seen blew across the schools. Education, as a social, religious and moral question came to the fore in the minds of thinking men by the 1860s and 70s in a way that has scarcely been equalled in the twentieth century.

Prior to 1870 the schools represented an astonishing picture, ranging at one end from the dames' schools and ragged schools that provided some brief acquaintance with the three Rs to hungry urchins in the urban areas, to the joint-stock boarding schools and reconstructed grammar schools that would shortly harden into a distinct, exclusive, self-contained system of secondary education for the middle classes – the public schools. Lying between the extremes were a mass of elementary schools, nearly all the property of the churches, in which some steady improvements were taking place thanks to a scheme for Government aid and inspection introduced in 1846. In schools that came under inspection a grant was paid direct to a certificated teacher and he for his part was encouraged to train his brightest pupils as pupil-teachers, who could then go on for a two-year certificate course at a training college.

But practically none of the schools were free and in consequence a great many children never went into them. Those who did were often erratic in attendance. The 'Extracts from the Private Diary of the Master of a London Ragged School' published in 1850 and 1851 gives some idea of the children who came to a difficult school. 'In decency of behaviour or in respect for the teacher or in discipline of any kind, they are totally unparalleled. No school can possibly be worse than this, the very appearance of one's coat is to them the badge of class and respectability; for although they may not know the meaning of the word, they know very well, or at least feel, that we are the representatives of beings with whom they have ever considered themselves at war'. In this school the teacher's success – in getting the children to sing the doxology at the start of the day, for instance – came because the children 'have been frightened into subjection'.

In the elementary schools generally, however, the system of inspection and pupil-teachers enabled strides to be made in spite of the appalling ratio of trained teachers to pupils, which could be at least 1 : 100. The system of pupil-teachers, a refinement of the discredited monitorial system, effectively broke down the large groups and the pupil-teachers themselves could be quite efficient in their teaching role. But the aims of this education were limited to basic literacy and arithmetic. The qualifications for candidates to be pupil-teachers at 13 were laid down in 1846 as follows:

*To read with fluency, ease and expression; to write in a neat hand with correct spelling and pronunciation, a simple prose narrative slowly read to them; to write from dictation sums in the first four rules of arithmetic, simple and compound; to work them correctly, and to know the table of weights and measures; to point out the parts of speech in a simple sentence; to have an elementary knowledge of geography; (in schools connected with the Church of England) they will be required to repeat the Catechism, and to show that they understand its meaning and are acquainted with the outline of Scripture history. (The parochial clergyman will assist in this part of the examination. In other schools the state of religious knowledge will be certified by the managers); to teach a junior class to the satisfaction of the Inspector, girls should also be able to sew neatly and to knit.*

But if education for the working classes was groping forward in spite of malnutrition, poor attendance and many other obstacles, a handful of enterprising, God fearing heads was simultaneously creating a new concept of education for the middle classes – a concept that would influence British ideas of a secondary education long after the children of workers were coming forward to claim it. People like Arnold of Rugby, Pears of Repton, Thring of Uppingham were introducing a broader curriculum than the decadent classicism of the ancient universities, a new respect for learning, and a new appreciation of education as essentially concerned with the formation of character, based on the total control of a child's environment that boarding schools permit.

In this innovative era, before the onset of imperialism and the cult of athleticism, a man like Edward Thring, a founder of the Headmasters' Conference, devised the study system – small rooms in which boys could study on their own – and brought over a German to start music in his school. (He was also prepared to move the whole school to Wales after a typhoid outbreak in Uppingham and would not return until the local authorities had introduced a new water supply and sanitary drainage.) Yet the growth of the public schools often meant a loss to their localities, and particularly to their poor children. Many of the public schools were grammar schools which met the snobbery of their new clients by excluding the sons of local tradesmen and by reorganising their original charitable foundations. (The 'misuse of educational endowments' would be a battlecry for the trade union movement into the 20th century.) The HMC sprang into existence to mount a successful campaign against the first draft of the Endowed Schools Bill of 1869, which would have brought these public schools under the control of a Government backed council. As it was actually passed, this Act hastened the process by which endowed schools became independent places for children of the rich.

The 1850s and 1860s were a great period for inquiries into different parts of Britain's inchoate education system. But first came the 1847 inquiry into Welsh education which had this to say about teachers:

*'No person, really qualified for the office of schoolmaster by moral character, mental energy, amiability of temper, and proficiency in all the elementary branches of education, together with aptitude in imparting knowledge, will doom himself to the worst paid labour and almost the least appreciated office to be met with in the country. Were even the means of training schoolmasters as ample as they are defective, and were the number of men adequately trained to the work at hand, the generality of schools would be not one jot the better supplied, for such training would fit men for employment in other spheres, where they would realise four or five times the emolument and enjoy a much higher social position than they can hope for as*

*schoolmasters in Wales under existing circumstances'.*

In 1852–3 came reports on Oxford and Cambridge. The Oxford report remarked in passing, 'of existing evils the most obvious are sensual vice, gambling in its various forms and extravagant expenditure . . . In the villages round Oxford . . . the opportunities to vice are too abundant . . .' In 1861 came the report of the Duke of Newcastle's Commission 'to inquire into the state of popular education in England'; The Earl of Clarendon's report on nine of the oldest public schools came in 1864; Lord Taunton's report on all those schools not covered by either Newcastle or Clarendon – mostly endowed or grammar schools – completed the series in 1868.

Of these unprecedented scrutinies, which set a fashion for major public inquiries into education which runs through to Newsom, Robbins and Plowden in more recent years, the one that mattered most for the certificated teachers was naturally the Newcastle report. The very establishment of the commission arose from dissatisfaction with the 1846 arrangements, some of which boded ill for the certificated teachers whose position had steadily advanced on this basis. Tropp, in *The School Teachers*, identifies at least six sets of critics: there were those who complained that popular education was not advancing fast enough, those who complained that state-aided elementary schools were enabling poor children to get a better education than the middle classes; those who complained that the certificated teachers were 'over educated' and becoming too ambitious socially; those nonconformists who wanted to curb the local educational monopolies of the Established Church; those who disliked the centralisation of the Committee of Council on Education and state interference; and those, including Gladstone and Bright who had a strangely modern concern for 'the growing burden of the government grant for education'.

The Newcastle commission relied considerably on the statistical evidence and views collected by ten assistant commissioners who toured the country. But when it came to writing the report it selected only such evidence and opinion as would suit its own prejudices. For broadly the evidence discounted the allegations of 'over-education' in the schools, supported the 1846 arrangements, and only attacked them because there were still substantial numbers of children and schools (especially small rural schools) that had failed to benefit. (Interestingly enough the commission found that the proportion of children in school to the whole population was not much worse in this country than in oft praised Prussia, where education was alleged to be compulsory, and it was higher than in Holland or France.)

Half the assistant commissioners found evidence of dissatisfaction, particularly among younger teachers, over their 'social position'. This was perhaps inevitable, as essentially the certificated teachers were able working class people who were claiming professional status in a new, Government subsidised occupation. But only one assistant commissioner saw this discontent as in any way

dangerous. In general the assistant commissioners were laudatory of the certificated teachers as a group, comparing them favourably with other teachers at the time. But the one fact that did emerge to discredit the teachers, on which a large part of the subsequent reaction was to hinge, was that the assistant commissioners were almost unanimous in agreeing that the elements of instruction were badly taught. Although the same researchers offered several reasons for this phenomenon, at least partly absolving the teachers themselves – for example shortage of teachers and truancy among the children – these were lost sight of.

The Newcastle Report heralded a tremendous educational disaster. One salient passage ran as follows:

*'The children do not, in fact, receive the kind of education they require. We have just noticed the extravagant disproportion between those who receive some education and those who receive a sufficient education. We know that the uninspected schools are in this respect far below the inspected; but even with regard to the inspected, we have seen overwhelming evidence from Her Majesty's Inspectors, to the effect that not more than one-fourth of the children receive a good education. So great a failure in the teaching demanded the closest investigation; and as the result of it we have been obliged to come to the conclusion that the instruction given is commonly both too ambitious and too superficial in its character, that (except in the very best schools) it has been too exclusively adapted to the elder scholars to the neglect of the younger ones, and that it often omits to secure a thorough grounding in the simplest but most essential parts of instruction . . .'*

This report is a good illustration of the thesis that reports of this kind are always an unsteady compromise between the observed facts, the opinions of the reporters, and the public demand they are designed to satisfy. The above declaration is a classic summary of the conservative, privileged view of British educational problems, an invisible thread that links the 1860s with the Black Paper debate over a century later. Its assumptions are that there is a particular kind of education appropriate to working class children, that younger children and 'a thorough grounding' are neglected, and that teachers are conspiring in an incompetence of monstrous proportions – a package which has the socially convenient result of restricting the products of the education commended to those stations in life which gentlemen disdain. It is also cavalier with facts – the 'overwhelming evidence' about 'one-fourth of the children' derived from the calculation of one HMI, which he later admitted should have come out as a half.

But more was at stake in 1861 than just the current performance of the schools or teachers. For the Newcastle Report concluded:

*'There is only one way of securing the results, which is to institute a searching examination by competent authority of every child in every school to which grants are to be paid, with the view of ascertaining whether these indispensable elements of knowledge are thoroughly acquired, and to make the prospects and position of the teacher dependent, to a considerable extent, on*

*the results of the examination'.*

On this foundation, in an even more wounding fashion for the teachers, schools and children, Mr Robert Lowe, vice president of the Council, was to create the Revised Code whose system of 'payment by results' was to endure for more than thirty years.

Speaking to the House of Commons Mr Lowe made the splendid assertion that 'I cannot promise the House that this system will be an economical one and I cannot promise that it will be an efficient one, but I can promise that it shall be one or the other. If it is not cheap it shall be efficient; if it is not efficient it shall be cheap'. (In fact, after rising sharply from £150,000 in 1851 to £836,920 in 1859 the Government education grant had already dropped to £813,441 in 1861, the year before the Revised Code appeared; it had fallen to £636,806 by 1865.)

In theory the system, which appealed to a utilitarian age, was a simple device to get better value for less money. Its proponents saw other merits too – that it would make teachers concentrate on the weaker pupils as they all had to reach a certain standard annually before grants could be awarded. Lowe himself also saw it as a covert method of aiding secularisation in the schools and avoiding the denominational obstructions. But in the controversy over the Code, which teachers denounced at once on a variety of scores, it was clear that class prejudice and emotional resentments were at work. Teachers were attacked for their 'vested interest' – particularly dirty words in the vocabulary of laissez faire economics – and even Lowe said that they were only concerned with their augmentation grants and they had been raised far above their true position in society.

Aside from the educational objections to the Code, the certificated teachers suffered immediately in themselves. Although, by nine votes in the Commons, the employment of certificated teachers by school managers as a condition for their receipt of a Government grant was upheld, the teachers lost their direct payments from Whitehall. In future all payments were to go to the managers, an arrangement that naturally increased teachers' dependence on them and put paid to the possibility that teachers might become civil servants, as happened to many of their European counterparts. Teachers and pupil-teachers engaged under the 1846 dispensation complained again and again that Lowe was breaking the agreement on which they had been recruited – namely, that they would have £15 to £30 annual augmentation grants, paid to them direct. At the same time the prospect of a Government supported pension, which had been held out ever since 1846, was now callously withdrawn.

At this point the weakness and divisions of the fragmented groups of teachers that then existed gravely hindered the attempts made to fight the Code. Although the Metropolitan Church Schoolmasters' Association and the London Association of Teachers agreed in September, 1861 to form a 'central committee of schoolmasters' the Associated Body of Church Schoolmasters, for example, preferred to operate on its own. Teachers and educational journals put up a spirited case. The London central committee sent a deputation to Lord Palmerston and got 2416 signatures to a memorial of protest. The ABCS, whose membership put on a spurt, got 4519 signatures to its petition to Parliament. A few concessions were made to the critics of the Code, but Lowe was substantially victorious. Had the teachers possessed an effective, representative organisation, the result might have been somewhat different. But, in the bleak aftermath of the Code, the defeated, bitter certificated teachers – the acknowledged cream of their profession – took this lesson to heart.

What did 'payment by results' mean in the schools? It meant the end of any attempt to teach outside the three Rs, and it ensured that these basics were taught in the most mechanical, least flexible manner possible. Reading, writing and arithmetic were reduced to six standards, through which children from the age of six up were expected to advance by annual examinations. Standard one in reading was the ability to manage a narrative in monosyllables; in writing, the ability to form capital or small letters from dictation on a blackboard or slate; in arithmetic, the ability to form numbers up to 20 from dictation and to name them, and to add or subtract figures up to ten. Standard six involved reading and writing a short ordinary paragraph in a newspaper, and calculating 'a sum in practice or bills of parcels'.

Throughout its early life the National Union of Elementary Teachers was fighting against 'payment by results', and over the years some modifications were achieved in subsequent codes. Among particular grievances were the 'music fine' – for anything taught outside the six standards represented a loss for the school managers – and the principle of grouping by age. Brighter children were held back and dull ones were coerced in order to reach the required levels. Endless drilling of young children, liberally supported by corporal punishment, were therefore imposed on the schools in those crucial decades in which education in the United Kingdom was rapidly extending and seeking to become universal. It was an extraordinary sacrifice of education to a shortsighted view of finance, converting working class children into the recalcitrant or deadened products of schools made into factories; even contemporary foreigners thought it was odd.

Because of the desperate importance of satisfying the inspectors – and up to two-thirds of a school's grant depended on these exams – teachers became accomplices in innumerable tricks and dodges. They would inform each other of the habits of particular inspectors, convey information to their children by signs like a card sharper, force children who could not read to memorise relevant passages, and avoid taking in those who were likely to fail to reach the necessary standards. The humiliation that these things involved for that minority of teachers who were qualified, who had been striving to cultivate a more enlightened view of education ever since 1846, may be readily imagined.

In 1889, when 'payment by results' was on its deathbed, the union was to summarise its objections in a memorial to Lord Salisbury, the Prime Minister, as follows: it had failed to provide the children with a good education; it had set up a false gauge of efficiency; it had necessitated a 'system of cram which encourages mechanical rather than intellectual methods of teaching', it had hurt both the bright and the slow; it had created suspicion between inspectors, managers and teachers; it condemned poor schools to continued inefficiency; and it had forced the same curriculum on all schools irrespectively.

More telling, perhaps, is the crossexamination of a woman who had been an assistant in a poor school. Mr R. Wild, a former president of the union, quoted from her evidence to an inquiry by the London School Board in a lecture he gave at the annual conference in 1903.

Q. *'Would there be children in those days in that infants' school who, because of the neglect of their early education, and because of the fact that they had only just been admitted to your school, could not possibly pass standard one at seven years of age? A. They did. We made them, they had to. Q. Do you care to describe to the committee the methods by which you made them? A. That is the reason I did not wish to continue in an elementary school. I could not continue such methods. Q. What were they? A. Coercion – driving. I used to keep the children in till one o'clock nearly every day – little children who had not enough to eat, or any wholesome blood in their bodies, so that their brain could work, day after day – day after day. And I used to stand over them until they did read. Q. You ultimately got them to pass? A. Yes'.*

But if the effects of 'payment by results' were painfully drawn out: the climate of hostility to the schools of 1862 gave way fairly soon to an atmosphere of optimism which produced both the Forster Education Act and the birth of the Union in 1870. It is of course a recurring pattern in English education that even the blackest reactions may yield some benefits, and in this case it may well be that the invention of a weapon that satisfied prevailing financial orthodoxy while providing the limited education thought necessary for poorer children made it safe to extend such an education throughout the country. Other factors, such as the widening of the suffrage by the 1867 Reform Act, contributed to the feeling that there must be a change.

While W. E. Forster, a Quaker Radical who was son-in-law to Thomas Arnold and brother-in-law to Matthew – hence intimately connected to some of the most creative Victorian educators – steered through his Bill, the teachers were playing a lively part in the controversies that surrounded it. The Act provided for elected School Boards to fill the gaps in the church school network, and laid down non-denominational religious teaching in the School Board schools. But it did not make schools free, nor attendance compulsory.

In the ferment of debates, with a National Education League vieing with a National Education Union, all contestants wanted to hear the views of teachers and they themselves realised the advantages of a united voice. After the letdown in 1862, in which teacher salaries had suffered, the multiple associations had come under attack and lost members. But by 1868 the ABCS, with J. J. Graves – the first president of the NUET – as its general secretary, was gathering new members. A London Association of Church Teachers was formed in the same year to assist the Church of England in its pressure over the forthcoming Bill and by March, 1870 this Association, with the Wesleyan and British Associations, was able to agree a common policy. The three groups held a conference with 13 Liberal MPs in April in which they advised that nonsectarian religious teaching was practical, but that there should be a conscience clause for children to opt out.

Throughout 1869 and early 1870 the associations had been considering schemes of union and the experience of common action, combined with the arrival of an Act which provided a new employer and, hopefully, a lessening of religious dissensions in the schools, gave the necessary final push. A meeting of about a hundred teachers at King's College, London gathered on June 25 'for the purpose of taking steps to bring about a union among elementary teachers throughout England'. According to legend a young man called George Collins made a crucial speech which ensured that a union was set up but probably William Lawson, the first secretary, was the most active figure behind the scenes. The first officers were Graves as president, J. Langton vice-president, J. H. Devonshire as treasurer and Lawson as secretary. The first topics to which the union promised to devote itself would be the revision of the code, the working of the Education Act, the establishment of a pensions scheme, the throwing open of higher educational offices to elementary teachers, and the proposal to obtain professional status by means of a public register of duly qualified teachers.

A student being examined before a large audience at St. Mark's College, Chelsea, soon after it was opened by the National Society in 1840.

21

# Teachers find new employers as local control is introduced

The School Boards introduced local democratic control into education for the first time. Members of the Boards were directly elected by the ratepayers, so that the teachers became employed by the public they served. A total of 2,568 School Boards were set up, most of them in towns. In the 30 years following 1870, elementary education predictably proved much more expensive than originally envisaged. The voluntary bodies strained every nerve to keep up with the rate-aided Boards. They got deeply in debt, while the Boards were increasingly attacked for extravagance. Opposition to *ad hoc* education authorities grew.

1

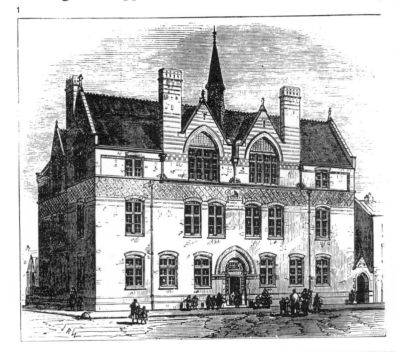

2

3

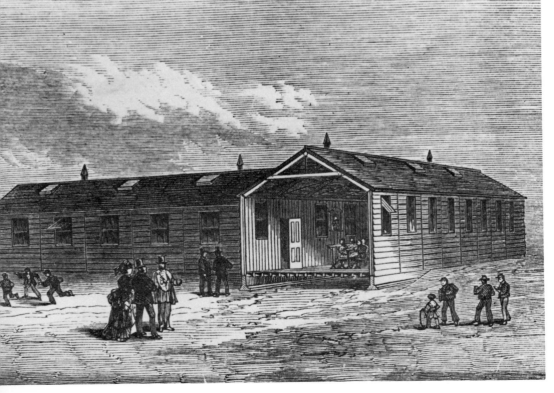

1 and 2. After 1870 Board schools sprang up all over the country. Most of them are still in use. The London Board was regarded as a pioneer in its architectural designs and Harper Street School in Lambeth is a good example of the style. The original building is still going strong as the Joseph Lancaster Primary School.

3. The Boards found it difficult to build enough schools fast enough. The Liverpool Board adopted the modern solution of prefabricated, movable, buildings.

B.ARNARD

4

# Leicester School Board Election,

*MONDAY NEXT, December 6th, 1897.*

## To the Burgesses of the Borough of Leicester.

LADIES AND GENTLEMEN,

Having been adopted by the Independent Labour Party as a candidate for the School Board, I beg respectfully to solicit your Vote and Interest on their behalf. I am not new to Educational Work, having served a term of nine months on the Leicester School Board. I regard the principal of Labour representation on all public bodies as a just and legitimate right, therefore I take this opportunity of making the influence of labour felt and respected on our local School Board; our hope as a nation lies in the correct education of the children of the workers, and it is of vital importance that we should, individually and collectively, do our utmost to secure the best possible education for them. I am a Trade Unionist of eleven years' standing; my whole life has been spent in the building trade, and as a practical man I should be of great service on the Building Committee.

I am in favour of abolishing theological teaching and substituting for it systematic moral instruction.

Having come in personal contact with the sufferings of our poor, I should urge the Board to endeavour to obtain the power to give at least one free meal per day to needy children.

I should advocate the appointment, by the Board, of Medical Gentlemen in various districts to examine children, as required by the Board, and grant Certificates free of expense.

I am in favour of Higher Grade Schools being provided for the advanced scholars, so that the children of the poor may have equal opportunities with those who are better off.

I think that facilities should be given for Lessons in Swimming for both sexes, and that the physical development of the children should receive attention as well as the intellectual.

I should advocate the Board doing its own work direct without the intervention of a contractor, and thus save the extortionate sums of money which flow into the pockets of contractors, and that only practical men be appointed as Clerks of Works.

I am in favour of the enforcement of a penalty for any evasion of the Board's terms of contract.

I am in favour of all employees under the Board retaining their citizenship and being free to organise or to take any public position, providing such does not interfere with their duties.

I am also in favour of Evening Sittings of the Board, in order to give greater facilities to working men to act as representatives.

Should you honour me with your support, I trust my devotion to my duties as a representative during the next three years will justify the confidence you repose in me.

I remain, yours faithfully,

85, St. Saviour's Road.

### HENRY PAYNE.

4 and 5. The system of electing Boards was surprisingly experimental. They were directly elected by ratepayers and women not only had the vote but could be elected; many of them were. Each voter had as many votes as there were candidates, so that they could 'plump' for one candidate. This gave minorities a chance to gain representation. The emergent Left-wing bodies of the SDF and ILP tried out their wings in School Board elections, with some success. Elections were hard-fought affairs arousing intense political passions, especially after 1895 when Lord Salisbury called on churchmen to 'capture the School Boards'. Henry Payne's election address is full of insights into the work of the Boards. Among other proposals he wanted teachers to sit on Boards, which was forbidden by a regulation of 1875.

# PLUMP FOR PAYNE!

## 15 VOTES.     NO CROSSES.

Printed and Published by the Leicester Co-operative Printing Society Limited, East Bond Street.

1. Fears were often expressed that the lower classes were being educated 'beyond their station.' Jargon changes, but a near modern equivalent is 'more means worse'.

2. Boards had quasi-judicial powers to enquire into non-attendance. Attendance Committees performed the same function for voluntary schools in each district.

3. Debate within the school boards was often highly acrimonious, giving good copy to the sensational press of the day. Here *The Day's Doings* tut-tuts about a 'disgraceful row' at West Hartlepool.

2                    3

## The London School Board sets the pace

4. The London Board was set up by a special Act of Parliament since its problems were unique. It led the way in many important fields; pioneered the use of a secret ballot; enforced compulsory attendance; and developed new ideas in teacher-training. J. W. Walton's picture shows the 53 members of the first London Board, including two ladies, being addressed by the chairman, Lord Lawrence. Many outstanding people sat on the Board.

## The London reformers

5. Elizabeth Garrett-Anderson, the woman who broke through the barriers against her sex in the field of medicine.

6. The 6th Marquess of Londonderry. He was chairman of the Board from 1895–7, and became President of the Board of Education in Balfour's Government.

7. Sydney Webb. As chairman of the London Technical Education Board he introduced a scholarship system that was adopted nationally after 1902.

8. Thomas Huxley, the famous scientist. He sat on the first Board and shaped the scheme of religious education.

# Teachers campaign to end child labour

With the demand for child labour continuing, many children were still employed after 1870. A campaign to amend the Factory Acts was one of the earliest and most vigorous conducted by the Union. In 1874 the minimum age for full-time employment was raised from 13 to 14.

1. A young boy working a machine for making shoe-laces.

2. Conditions in the brickfields were particularly harsh.

3. Half-timers leaving a Lancashire mill for a few hours of schooling. The system of half-timers (half-time at school, half at work) proved more intractable. It was a truce situation to meet the demands of certain employers, mainly the millowners of Lancashire and Yorkshire and the farmers of East Anglia. The minimum age was raised from 10 to 11 in 1891 (again partly through Union pressure) but the system lingered on until 1918.

4. Parents were not always quick to appreciate the advantages of full-time schooling against the loss of extra wages.

5. A group of cheerful shoeblacks in Liverpool.

3

4

5

# 'We can't learn, sir, we're starving'

The introduction of fully compulsory education in 1880 brought many more children to school for the first time. It soon became apparent that their poor physical condition was a major barrier to learning. In the 1890's Charles Booth published his monumental survey, *Life and Labour in London*, which for the first time demonstrated the extent of the problem of poverty.

1. A Punch cartoon summed up the situation neatly. The boy is asking 'Please, sir, mayn't we have summat to relieve the craving of 'unger fust?'

2. Health services were limited to cleaning up the children. Often schools were shut for weeks because of an epidemic.

3. A 'penny dinner' for Board school children. Charitable bodies were beginning to provide meals, but as yet no official action was taken.

# The Union's first campaigns

The Forster Act set off an unprecedented burst of school building, and a consequent expansion of the teacher force which the Union, ably led from the beginning, used to consolidate its position and to press for educational improvements. (Before examining the growth of the union in detail in these years it is worth having a look at the broad sweep of educational developments.)

'Next to the Eastern Question', said Mr W. Gardner, president of the Union in 1877, 'the question of Education is undoubtedly the question of the day. It has been dealt with by men of every shade of opinion, political and religious. It forms one of the chief topics of almost every public speech'. In this atmosphere of enthusiasm the new School Boards and the church authorities took off in an orgy of competitive school building. Pressing on the School Boards were the nonconformists, often in political alliance with the Liberal Party, who were hostile to the idea of sending their children to Anglican schools; at the same time the Boards could count on the support, which became increasingly important towards the close of the century, of working class organisations like the trade unions which generally supported nonsectarian, popularly controlled schools.

On the other side the Anglican drive to extend the voluntary schools was equally understandable. In the eyes of the Bishops the church was in danger of losing its influence on education – particularly dangerous if this meant that the working class was to be lost to secularism. (In this period too there was a real fear that the Church of England might be disestablished.) But the Anglicans, informally cooperating with the Conservative Party, found themselves constantly lagging behind the superior resources of the Boards, backed by the rates. It was a continual grievance to the Church that the faithful had to pay twice – once for the school rates and once by levy for the voluntary schools. In these circumstances the Anglicans resorted to attempts to capture the School Boards with the twin objectives of keeping their rates and enterprise on a tight rein and, where possible, of inserting religious tests in the Board schools. By the 90s, when the position of the voluntary schools was getting increasingly untenable, Bishop Fox of Birmingham carried out a successful putsch on the city's School Board – where Chamberlainites had long repressed religious teaching – and the celebrated Rev. J. R. Diggle, chairman of the London School Board, attempted to impose a theological test on teachers.

In one year in the early 70s accommodation for children in schools rose by a sixth. In that decade the School Boards started or took over between 3000 and 4000 schools while the number of voluntary schools rose from 8000 to 14000. But the sharp disparity in standards between the rival systems is indicated by the following figures: whereas between 1870 and 1895 the School Boards provided new accommodation for 2,211,299 children for £29,468,477, the voluntary schools, between 1870 and 1891, built places for 1,475,000 for only £7m. By 1900 there were almost as many children in Board Schools as in the voluntary ones.

From the point of view of the Union this unequal struggle, which was reflected in variations of teacher salaries and marked differences between urban and rural standards, was no cause for delight. By training and outlook many of the certificated teachers were religious men, and Anglicans. But however much they disliked it they found themselves in a position where, as Mr Allen Croft, the Union's president in 1902 explained, nearly two-thirds of the certificated teachers were in Board schools while over four-fifths of the Article 68 assistant teachers (basically untrained women) were in voluntary schools. By then the Board schools together had five times more income in rates that the voluntary schools were able to win from sources that ranged down to church bazaars.

Broadly speaking the teachers found, following the 1870 Act, that their best employers were the larger School Boards. Both the small Boards and the voluntary managers – particularly rural parsons – could be downright tyrannical. Whereas far sighted and enthusiastic people might be elected to the School Boards, like T. H. Huxley in London or Margaret McMillan, the famous ILP campaigner for free meals and medical inspection, in Bradford, ill educated and narrow minded people might also have oversight of the Board schools. One London head teacher, who was under attack from some of his managers for refusing to go beyond the syllabus of religious instruction laid down by the School Board, made the mistake of leaving a degree textbook on physiology on his desk during the lunch hour. A prudish woman manager spotted the book and engineered a nasty correspondence in the local press. One letter went, 'Sir, We were informed that our poor children were to be taught reading, writing and arithmetic only. Now this schoolmaster teaches them the contents of their own insides and thus adds to the rudeness which is innate in the lower orders. If the Author of the Universe had meant us to know what our livers are like he would not have hidden them away in security'.

The worst aspect of this kind of management was that teachers were often dismissed capriciously. In the countryside, for example, where the rector and schoolteacher formed the local cultural establishment, a considerable number of clergymen held the view that an incoming parson had the right to dismiss the head of his voluntary school. Even the *Church Times*, on December 15, 1894, recognised the injustice that was involved. 'There is one point of clerical conduct which demands serious attention. We refer to the autocratic and unjust treatment to which the masters of parish schools too frequently have to submit', it stated, adding that teachers should have a court of appeal.

Mr Marshall Jackman, president of the Union in 1900, said that it was having to deal with tenure cases at a rate that suggested that some 60 per cent of teachers might need some advice in the course of a working lifetime. In his presidential address he listed a number of scandals that had been referred to the union. A master of 16 years' service, for instance, was asked to sign a new agreement which meant a loss of £20 a year in salary. At first the vicar denied that there was any reduction, but then he had to admit that there was. 'He said he wanted the money for repairing the roof of the church', added Mr Jackman. One teacher was dismissed because she refused to attend early communion, another because he had tried to get rid of an incompetent Article 68 teacher, who happened to be the verger's daughter. In the same address, in a pardonable slip into Victorian sentimentality, he mentioned a Southport teacher who had gone to 'a premature grave' because of the worry of a tenure battle, and of a wife who had committed suicide. ('Never lived a better man', she wrote, 'truly a martyr. How shockingly treated . . . Father, be good to my boys. Dear Mamma, see Fred through . . .'.)

Dismissal for an older certificated teacher, at a time when there was a glut of Article 68 teachers who could be employed more cheaply, could mean utter ruin, and one of the chief services of the union to its members at this period was that it fought tenure cases energetically. The union took legal action where necessary; in some cases, by investigating the original trust deeds, it was able to reform a board of managers; at Brighton and Cockermouth, by lobbying and a public campaign, it managed to capture the School Boards that had dismissed teachers at the triennial elections; at Southampton it got a dismissed teacher elected to the School Board; and at Richmond, after a Mr Whittaker had been fired, it took the ultimate step of building a new school for him.

Although the Boards were empowered to make attendance compulsory it was not until 1880 that attendance was made compulsory throughout the country. Even then there was one notable loophole, the 'half-time' system, which was particularly popular in the Lancashire cotton towns; under this arrangement, which derived from the Factory Acts, children could leave school for half-time employment at the age of ten, or 11 after 1893. The effect on young teenagers, made to attend school and do the repetitive work of the factories, was pitiful. Ben Turner recalled it as follows,

'The day I was ten years of age, I went into the mill as a half-timer. We had to go to school one half-day and the mill the other half-day. One week we started work at 6 am and went on to 12.30 pm with a half hour for breakfast. We then had to go to school from 2 to 4.30 pm. The opposite week we went to school at 9 am until 12 noon, and to work from 1.30 pm until 6 pm. It was a bit cruel at times when on the morning turn at the mill – for it meant being up at 5 am, getting a drop of something warm, and trudging off to the mill a mile away to begin work. In winter it was fearful'.

At the same time, in country areas, there were similar abuses. When he wanted youngsters to do some potato picking a farmer, who might himself be a voluntary school manager, would find it more economic to pay a school attendance fine than to find other labour. Efforts to secure a better and more regular attendance were a prime educational objective of the union in its early years. J. H. Devonshire, president in 1875, pointed out then that it was ridiculous that after such an impressive school building programme nearly half the school places were unoccupied. Absenteeism in Board schools was running at 40 per cent at that time. 'A London school, opened between two and three years ago', he said, 'has admitted, up to this present time, considerably over 2,000 scholars, and the average attendance is a little over 400. What this means no-one but the teacher fully knows. A constant stream of incomers, a constant stream of outgoers, the scholars must have changed on an average at least every three months'.

Closely related to the attendance problem was the fact that, until the 1891 'Free Education' Act and in some schools for longer, parents were obliged to pay fees for their children's elementary schooling – the 'school pence'. Fees varied from about 2d to 8d a week, but they were sufficient to add to the hardships of a large family at the worst point of a trade cycle. Councillor Threllfall, president of the Trades Union Congress in 1885 – a bad year in many manufacturing districts – said that for a family with an income of 15s to 18s a week and four children the school pence could result in a drastic limiting of spending on food and clothing. 'Under proper conditions education would be hailed with joy, but School Board experience will show that the Elementary Education Acts are regarded with hatred, and are constantly evaded by thousands of families', he said. The delay between making attendance compulsory and providing that it could be free seems curious to modern eyes: but Victorian views on the financial responsibility of a family, and the dependence of impecunious voluntary schools on fees, go far to explain it.

But it is appropriate now to look at the growth of the Union rather more closely. 'We inaugurate in founding this "National Union of Elementary Teachers", no aggressive association. We desire to assail nobody. We do desire to think and act as reasonable and educated men, to advocate improvements in our educational schemes and machinery, to look after the welfare of the nation as far as elementary education affects it, and at the same time try to advance our own interests, convinced that by the elevation of the teacher, we elevate the value of education, and accelerate the progress of civilisation', said the president, J. J. Graves, in 1870. In this spirit, eschewing the principles of militant trade unionism put forward by the Nottingham association, the Union set out on its eventful history

This first presidential outlined several of the issues the Union was to take up firmly. Graves pointed out, for instance, that although the 1870 Education Act was generally welcome it said nothing about how enough properly trained and qualified teachers were to be found for the new schools. He feared that the standard of the certificate would be lowered and looked forward to a consolidated educational system in which children from elementary schools could go to universities, and in which elementary teachers could be masters of grammar schools. He wanted the union to fight for a pensions scheme, to make it possible for elementary teachers to be appointed to the inspectorate; he supported compulsory schooling and the teaching of nonsectarian religion.

The lowering of the value of the certificate to cater for the expanding demand for

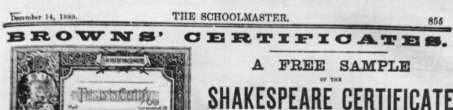

A page of advertisements from *The Schoolmaster* in 1889.

30

teachers naturally riled those who had earned one when it was a real mark of excellence. The campaign to win some control of entry into the profession – conducted in the twentieth century through such agencies as the National Advisory Council for the Training and Supply of Teachers – was well begun in the 19th century. After the initial setback of the Revised Code, when teacher salaries dropped and the number of pupil-teachers fell, the 1870 Act led to a doubling of the number of pupil-teachers in five years. A deputation was sent to Forster to complain. In 1878 T. E. Heller, then the general secretary, told the union conference that 'the power of controlling the entrance into the profession must be placed in the hands of an independent representative body under the control of Parliament, and the teacher's diploma must be placed beyond the caprice or the necessities of a government department'.

In 1879 union pressure secured that a Bill sponsored by the College of Preceptors, which would specifically have debarred elementary teachers from registration while opening a register for those in middle class schools, was withdrawn in the Commons. Pressure on the Education Department achieved some success in the 1880 code in closing side entrances to the profession, and thereafter there was a continuing effort to reduce the number of unqualified teachers and to raise the standard of the certificate. But the majority report of the Cross Commission, appointed by a Conservative Government, did not favour the Union's position when it appeared in 1888.

The Union, in spite of sympathy in the Education Department, did not get very far in this campaign in the 19th century. Because of the light they shed on the psychology of the union at the turn of the century – as an elite minority of teachers promoting working class education – it is worth studying the figures for the teaching force in 1899. In that year there were only 62,000 certificated teachers and about 80,000 others. Of the certificated teachers, two thirds of whom were Union members, there were 24,000 men (69·3 per cent trained for two years, 28·1 per cent untrained) and nearly 38,000 women (46·5 per cent trained for two years, 50·9 per cent untrained). Of the uncertificated lump there were 30,000 assistant teachers, many of whom would be preparing for the certificate exam, nearly 17,000 additional women teachers (the Article 68 group who needed only to be 18 plus, and to be vaccinated and to satisfy an HMI), nearly 31,000 pupil-teachers, and about 2,500 probationers.

Another campaign by the Union, which was fed by deep feeling, aimed to throw open the Inspectorate to elementary teachers. Before the Revised Code, when the great majority of inspectors were clergyman who had taken up the cause of popular education, the relations between HMIs and teachers were generally friendly and their cooperation was fruitful. But the Code turned them into hostile parties and the policy after 1870, to appoint young university men with often no better qualification than a claim on political patronage, introduced class antagonism also. Although the Cross Commission believed that

elementary teachers should have a chance of this profitable promotion, and there seemed in the 80s some hope that they would succeed through the half-way stage of a Sub Inspectorate, the union suffered a setback in 1901 when the Inspectorate was reorganised and recruitment was clearly restricted to Oxbridge products.

Given the powers over teachers of managers and HMIs and the severe penalty involved in a suspension or cancellation of the teacher's certificate it was a continuing aim of the Union to obtain a fair right of appeal. Anger was aroused in 1877 when the department started to publish a black list of teachers whose certificates were in question, although the teachers concerned had had no opportunity of answering charges of drunkenness, immorality and so on. Hence the Union was encouraged to launch a public fight over the case of Mr R. E. H. Goffin, head of the United Westminster Schools, and a member of the Union's executive. His certificate was withdrawn in 1878 after he had been accused by the Science and Art Department of having obtained exam. papers and then passing the information to his pupils.

Although the Union concentrated on the need for an inquiry, rather than on the innocence of Mr Goffin, it was highly embarrassed when a Parliamentary Select Committee set up after the outcry decided that the original verdict was just. However in 1880 the Department promised that no certificate would be cancelled or suspended until the teacher had been informed of the charges and had had a chance to explain himself. By the end of the century an effective informal consulation system had been established between the union and the department in all such cases.

One of the greatest victories on a point embodied in the pioneers' manifesto of 1870 was finally achieved by legislation in 1898 – a national state-aided system of pensions for teachers. The way in which the Union, by persistent lobbying over decades, managed to resuscitate the 1846 Minute and convert it into a reality is an object lesson in pressure group politics. In 1872, within two years of the union's foundation, a decade after the Revised Code had swept away the hopes of 1846, the teachers had succeeded in getting a Select Committee set up to examine the possibility. Although the Committee's report was unhelpful the Committee of Council revived its pension scheme for entrants before 1862 in 1875; the final trigger that brought in superannuation throughout England and Wales for teachers in both Board and voluntary schools, was a Bill from the London School Board in 1891 and a tremendous campaign by the Union in the same year.

Throughout the 19th century there was one issue on which the union, which generally enjoyed the support of radical and advanced working class opinion, fell foul of its friends. This was the issue of corporal punishment. It was not until the publication of the Plowden Report in 1967 that abolition became a major talking point, but in the Victorian era it caused lively controversy. Jeremy Bentham, after all, had advocated abolition and later there were both School Boards that tried to

limit the infliction of caning in their schools and magistrates who were quick to penalise schoolteachers. Corporal punishment was one of the chief categories of 'causes of difficulty' for members with which the union had to deal.

Such punishment, as has been shown, was an integral part of the harsh regime with which the Revised Code endowed the schools, and HMIs from cane-happy public schools were not inclined to question it. The conventional view of the union at this time was given in a lecture to the 1890 conference by Dr Abbott, recent head of the City of London School. 'From an interesting report by Mr Fitch on American Schools, published last year, I learn that "in most of the state and city regulations teachers are absolutely forbidden to inflict it", and that is a point

T. J. Macnamara – a cartoon by 'Spy' in 1900.

worth considering . . . Under proper regulations, and in the hands of experienced and responsible teachers, the cane seems to me an institution for good in English schools as at present constituted; and if, as I believe, this is the general opinion not only of school teachers but also of school managers, it seems time that some pressure should be brought to bear upon those magistrates who set their face against caning under any circumstances'. The Union opposed attempts to restrict the right of corporal punishment to heads alone; though it disappointed progressive opinion at the time, its eventual victory in the war against 'payment by results' was a powerful shove in the same direction.

Dr Abbott's reference to 'pressure' was a recognition that in its first twenty years the Union had developed effective methods of making its views felt. From conferences with MPs, to public petitions, to lobbying at School Board elections – where a system of multiple voting allowed minorities considerable power – and to the remedies of legal action, an armoury of useful weapons had been built up. In 1872 the union had agreed to a paid secretary, it had a regular organ in *The Schoolmaster* (1d weekly, 'The only weekly paper entirely devoted to the interests of the scholastic profession') and, except during the hostile secretaryship of Patric Cumin (1884–90) the Union had good relations with the Education Department. In 1885 the union first attempted to sponsor its own MPs, a controversial procedure that was crowned with success in 1895 when the general secretary J. H. Yoxall (Liberal) and Ernest Gray (Conservative) were both elected. In the 90s too the Union started blacklisting schools in which teachers were forced to do extraneous duties, although a proposal to set up a sustentation fund to fight salary claims was defeated in a referendum.

Affiliation to the TUC was beaten by a two to one vote in 1895. Internally the progress of the Union was marked by a period of slow growth in the 1870s, followed by a crisis in the mid 80s, and a rapid advance in the 90s. Membership, which was nearly 5,000 in 1872, rose gradually, dipped in the 80s and stood at just over 16,000 in 1890; by 1900 there were 43,621 members of the Union. In 1889 the Union had changed its name, from the National Union of Elementary Teachers – which offended many on status grounds and no longer accurately described the work of some members – to the National Union of Teachers. (A short sighted proposal to call it the National Union of English Teachers was dropped after a patriotic campaign by Welsh members.)

William Lawson resigned as secretary in 1873, when he wrongly thought the conference was about to embark on a policy of militant trades unionism, and the secretaryship of T. E. Heller (1873–91) a church teacher corresponded to the phase of consolidation. The difficulties of the 1880s seem to have resulted from a variety of causes: the advancing age of the 'old guard' of the 1870s, the growing rifts between Board and voluntary teachers as the economic problems of the voluntary schools worsened, and the Parliamentary initiative in 1885 which made it appear that the union was lining itself up exclusively with the Liberal Party. A perennial difficulty was the friction between the relatively privileged London School Board teachers and other members of the Union. At times the London School Board was employing as many as a quarter of the certificated teachers in the country; from 1873, when all but one on the executive were London teachers (the outsider came from no further than Surbiton) until 1894, when almost half the executive were Metropolitan teachers, they formed a dominant group.

But if the 80s saw the growth of pressure groups within the Union, they also saw the start of a renewal. This was linked to the success of a band of teachers who described themselves as the 'Indefatigables'. Led by an exceptionally able pair, J. H. Yoxall (general secretary 1892–1924) and T. J. Macnamara, Editor of *The Schoolmaster* from 1892, a brilliant orator and a Liberal MP in 1900, they were responsible for the quick rise in membership, the strong stand taken by the union on a number of issues, and for steering teachers round the quicksands of the 1902 Act.

# Elementary schooling becomes free and compulsory

The 1880 Act, which made schooling compulsory up to the age of 10, included an arrangement which nicely illustrates the Victorian idea that elementary education was a measurable and strictly limited commodity. Children were allowed to leave at 10 if they had achieved a certain standard or even if they had only put in the required number of attendances; if not, they had to stay on until 13. By 1899 compulsion extended to the age of 12. School fees put a severe strain on parental resources, and the demand for free schooling became a torrent in the 1880's, supported by the Union. The voluntary schools did not want to forego fees, which put a major plank in their precarious financial structure. The 1891 Act allowed Board and voluntary schools to admit children free, and to claim a 'fee grant' from the Exchequer. The grant constituted a hidden subsidy to voluntary schools.

Theologians continued to argue about religious education, though the Union felt that parents were on the whole not much concerned. A few Boards provided a purely secular education, but most followed the example of Manchester in adopting a solution very similar to today's agreed syllabuses, by which local clergymen got together to work out a scheme.

4. A schoolroom in the 1890's. The children in the foreground are exercising with dumbbells. It was quite common to have a single large room housing the whole school, often divided by movable partitions. There might be only one qualified teacher, and he would concentrate on the older pupils while superintending pupil-teachers. The overall staffing ratio in 1897, even allowing for pupil-teachers, was 35 to 1.

5 and 6. A gallery class in the Chelsea Oratory Infants' School. A gallery for the youngest pupils was a standard feature, planned so that the teacher could see clearly what each infant was up to. Its static nature tellingly contrasts with the free classroom atmosphere in the same school today.

**Then and now**

4

5

6

1. A London School Board capture. The London Board was one of the first to compel attendance and to employ a 'Board's man' to round up unwilling pupils.

2. In 1883 the Union sent this circular letter to all local authorities complaining that in some districts the 1880 Act was not being enforced. It calls on 'all educational agencies' to 'work harmoniously together in securing the common object of their efforts, viz. an improved attendance at school.' The Union believed, rather idealistically, that a few years of strict compulsion would create an educated generation who would not need to be forced to come to school. Some magistrates were refusing to enforce the law, and some members of School Boards and Attendance Committees were in active opposition to it.

One cannot doubt the Union's belief in educational progress, but there were also good financial reasons why they should act strongly on attendance. Grants to schools were partly assessed by attendance figures and teachers were in the long run dependant on government grants. The letter points out that voluntary schools in rural districts were particularly threatened; attendance in some such schools was as low as 52 per cent.

The Union recommended to the Education Department the most specific actions to be taken, including a tightening-up of regulations relating to half-timers. It is a measure of the self-confidence the NUT had achieved. For the first few years of their existence they had to fight for any recognition from the Education Department. But the appointment of Mundella, a staunch friend of the Union, as Vice-President in 1880 was a turning-point, though they heartily disagreed with many of his actions.

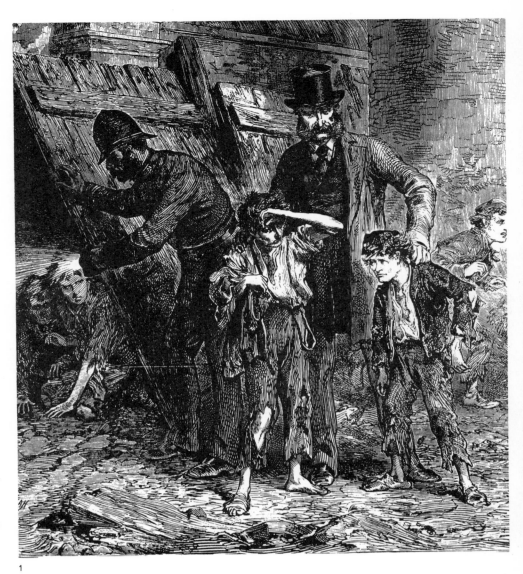

1

2

# National Union of Elementary Teachers.

## CIRCULAR LETTER TO LOCAL AUTHORITIES.

To the Clerk of the *Acdon*

{ School Attendance Committee.
—or—
School Board.

Sir,

During the past year the Executive of the National Union of Elementary Teachers have made a careful inquiry into the state of School Attendance in England and Wales, and have fully considered the reports received from a large number of Teachers' Associations in various parts of the country. The Executive instituted this inquiry in consequence of the increased importance of regular attendance under the New Code, and the numerous complaints received from Managers and Teachers as to the lax way in which many Local Authorities and Magistrates were applying the law relating to compulsory attendance at school. The attention of the Education Department has been already called to this question, and certain recommendations have been made with the object of securing a more efficient administration of the law.

I am now instructed to call the attention of the Local Authorities to the subject, and to suggest that a simultaneous effort should be immediately made by these bodies throughout England and Wales to secure a better average attendance of scholars. In this effort it is the earnest desire of the Teachers to co-operate, and it is hoped that all the educational agencies of the country, the religious bodies, Boards of Guardians, Magistrates, Local Authorities, and Attendance Officers may work harmoniously together in securing the common object of their efforts—viz., an improved attendance at school. In this spirit the present communication is made. The Executive of the National Union are of opinion that a few years of strict and careful administration of the Bye-Laws will remove

## The Oxfordshire collection

Oxfordshire County Council has a unique photographic record that gives a very good idea of the sort of country school being built in the second half of the 19th century by Boards and churches. These examples convey the atmosphere of the simple buildings, something in the style of the local churches. The classrooms were heated by cumbersome 'tortoise' stoves and lit by oil lamps. Glass partitions were much favoured. The water supply was usually a pump in the playground or even had to be carried from the village pump.

# The N U T fights for a wider curriculum

2. Some HMIs were against the 'payment by results' system which they had to administer. The most outspoken was Matthew Arnold, who called it 'a game of mechanical contrivance' in which children were 'forcibly fed with semi-digested food.'

The 'payment by results' system was introduced by the 1861 Revised Code. The government grant to a school was assessed by individual examination of each child, together with the level of attendance. The 'standard' to be reached was precisely laid down – hence the use of 'standard' to denote classes. It was based on a utilitarian notion that everything could be given a money value and it acted as a particularly tight strait-jacket on educational methods. To achieve the grant teachers had little choice but to drill their pupils into a mechanical facility. The NUT fought a long and bitter battle against the system, and its abolition in 1895 was one of the Union's major achievements in this period.

The contents of the curriculum began with a narrow insistence on the 3 Rs, but gradually broadened with the introduction of 'optional subjects' into a more liberal education. 'Class' subjects including geography and history could be taught above Standard I. 'Specific' subjects such as science were taught above Standard IV.

3. Inspection day was a trial for teachers and pupils. This song was a brave attempt to keep up their spirits.

### 1.

Would you like to know the reason
    Why we all look bright and gay
As we hasten to our places ?
    This is our Inspection Day !
*f*  Fie ! what is that you say,
    You hate Inspection Day ?

### 2.

*mf*  If we know we've done our duty,
    Daily striving with our might,
*cres.*  Teacher says we need not worry
    Though our sums will not come right.
*f*  So we are glad and gay,
    Though 'tis Inspection Day.

### Why teachers hated and feared the HMI

1. D. R. Fearon in a standard work on School Inspection in 1876 wrote that 'Education, unfortunately is an art, which is subject to so many delusions, that teachers whose work is not tested by examination as well as by inspection will be sure to deceive both themselves and the inspector.' The teachers regarded HMIs as their natural enemies – not surprising in the light of the power inspectors had over every aspect of their work. Their dislike was exacerbated by the fact that inspectors were Oxbridge men with no direct experience of elementary schools. The Union failed completely to achieve the promotion of teachers to the inspectorate. The pages of *The Schoolmaster* were full of complaints about inspectors, of which the most startling piece of invective is this attack by James Runciman on the Rev. D. J. Stewart. How much duller modern newspapers are under the present libel laws.

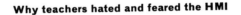

## MR. STEWART'S TESTIMONIAL.

### By James Runciman.

It surely cannot be true that any attempt will be made to present publicly a testimonial to the Rev. D. J. Stewart. His private friends may, if they like, make him a present, to show their regard ; but it would be stupid—it would be wicked—to make it appear that the Greenwich teachers, as a body, approve his conduct. When I think of the misery caused by that man, I find it hard to restrain myself. His cynical contempt for fairness and for common truthfulness made me indignant ; and I know, only too well, how many fine young fellows have been hindered in life through his lazy and haphazard mode of endorsing certificates. Why, that man would lounge round a school for ten minutes, and then go away to write the same mechanical report on the certificates of the whole staff ! In some cases, the parchment scribbled on by Mr. Stewart is about as valuable as a ticket-of-leave to its possessor. Then look at the insolence of his attitude towards teachers ; read the jeering accusations which he uttered before the Royal Commission ; and then say whether any feeling save solemn indignation should be made manifest toward him. He never damaged me, and I guess if he had tried it on once, he never would have repeated the operation ; but I saw him serve one of my assistants in a way whereof the memory makes my hands twitch to this day.

4. This advertisement sums up very well what elementary schooling was all about.

## Hartlepool Board School.

Head Master, - - Mr. WILLIAM McDONALD.
1st Assistant Master, - - Mr. H. BOWNASS.
2nd     do., - - Mr. H. C. MARSTON.
3rd     do., - - Mr. T. B. BUCKLE.
Drill Instructor, - - Mr. C. RAMSEY.
NO BOYS ARE EMPLOYED AS TEACHERS.

### SCHOOL FEES.

STANDARDS I., II., III., - - - 3d. per Week.
  Do. IV., V., VI., - - - 4d.   do.
A FAMILY, - - - 10d.   do.
*All Fees are payable in advance, and should be paid each Monday morning. Arrears are reported to the School Board when they amount to 2s. 6d. A dated receipt is given for each payment of school fees.*

### SUBJECTS OF STUDY.

ELEMENTARY—READING, WRITING, AND ARITHMETIC.
Advanced—GEOGRAPHY, GRAMMAR, DRAWING, THEORETICAL MUSIC, COMMERCIAL CORRESPONDENCE, CHEMISTRY OF COMMON THINGS, ENGLISH LITERATURE, HISTORY, AND COMPOSITION.
Special Subjects for Boys who have passed the Sixth Standard of Education.—
  LOGARITHMETICAL ARITHMETIC, EUCLID, ALGEBRA, MENSURATION, TRIGONOMETRY, DR. SMITH'S FIRST GREEK AND LATIN COURSES.
Forty Minutes is devoted each day to Scripture.

### PRIVATE LESSONS

MAY BE HAD IN NAVIGATION, NAUTICAL ASTRONOMY, DRAWING, THEORETICAL MECHANICS, MUSIC, AND MATHEMATICS.
The Head Teacher holds special advanced Government Certificates in these Subjects.

### HOURS OF ATTENDANCE.

Morning—Nine to Eleven-Thirty.     Afternoon—One-Thirty to Four-Thirty.
These hours facilitate dinner carrying.
*DOORS OPEN TEN MINUTES EARLIER FOR ASSEMBLY.*
Punctuality and Regularity are of importance to the progress of pupils individually, and the well-being of the School generally.

Birds, oh! Birds, ye are beautiful things.

With your earth-heading feet and cloud-cleaving wings.

Where shall man wander, and where shall he dwell.

Beautiful Birds! that ye come not as well!

Ye have nests on the mountain all rugged and stark.

Ye have nests in the forest all tangled and dark.

Ye build and ye brood 'neath the cottager's eaves.

And ye sleep on the sod 'mid the bonny green leaves.

**5.** Page of a copy-book. Great emphasis was laid on good handwriting and moral precepts.

**6.** Teachers lost a great deal of liberal sympathy by their insistence on the right to use corporal punishment, for even minor mistakes. But it was true that they had a very tough job.

5

6

and || Conjunction joining two words together
balm || Com. Noun. 3rd Sing. Num. Neut. Gend. Nom. Case governed by 'wept'
March 16th 187

8

7

9

**7.** Parsing was regarded as a very necessary exercise. Appreciation of literature was not so highly prized.

**8.** A 'discipline master' was a strange sort of specialist body. Note that he actually received less than the nightwatchman. Salary scales fluctuated wildly from district to district. The country schoolmaster in a voluntary school came off worst.

**9.** This Victorian text-book, though, has quite a modern thematic approach and is attractively designed.

Here are two bunches of cherries. — How many are there in the first? How many in the second? How many are 3 & 2? Of what colour are these cherries? What shape are they? What is inside a cherry? Of what use are cherries? Are they good? (5 = 3 + 2.)

If 2 out of 5 cups are broken how many remain? Tell me some other easily broken vessel? What is the use of cups? Who makes them? From whence are they made? (describe to the child how they are made.) (2 from 5 = 3, 5 times 1 = 5 = 5 times 1.)

# PUPIL TEACHER EXAMINATION PAPERS.

## CANDIDATES.

Three hours and a half allowed.

*Dictation.*

Write from dictation the passage given out by the Inspector.

*Grammar.*

Point out the parts of speech in the following lines, and, if you are able, *parse* the words:—

> If gems we seek we only tire,
> And lift our hopes too high,
> The constant flowers that line our way;
> Alone can satisfy.

*Arithmetic.*

Write down and work the sums dictated to you by the Inspector.

*Geography.*

1. Explain each word in the following passage printed in italics, and give examples in North Wales. Name the counties:—North Wales is a land of soaring *heights*, limited *plains*, narrow *vales*, and deep *ravines*. Its highest *peak* rises 3,751 feet above the *sea level*. The *mountains* are full of *minerals*. It is divided into six *counties*. The principal railway is that from Chester to *Holyhead*, crossing the Menai *Straits* by the famous *tubular bridge*.

2. Does a globe or a map of the world give the more correct view of it? Is either perfectly correct? Give reasons for your answer.

## END OF FIRST YEAR.

Three hours and a half allowed.

*Arithmetic.*

1. A person gives a £5 note to pay the following bill:—$3\frac{1}{2}$ cwt. of coals at $10\frac{1}{2}$d. a cwt.; 13 lbs. of cheese at $7\frac{3}{4}$d. a lb.; $2\frac{3}{4}$ lbs. of tea at 3s. 3d. a lb.; 17 lbs. of sugar at $5\frac{1}{2}$d. a lb.; $8\frac{1}{4}$ yards of flannel at 1s. $11\frac{1}{2}$d. a yard; and 29 yards of calico at $10\frac{3}{4}$d. a yard. What change should he receive?

2. Find, by practice, the value of 1 pipe 47 gal. 1 qt. of wine at £28 17s. 6d. a hogshead.

3. Find the value of $2{,}037\frac{1}{2}$ cwt. of sugar at £1 19s. $8\frac{1}{2}$d. a cwt.

4. Work by practice:—A bankrupt's debts amount to £3,548 6s. 8d., what will his creditors lose if he pays 12s. $10\frac{1}{2}$d. in the pound?

*Grammar.*

1. Give instances of verbs which do not change their form for the perfect tense and the passive participle.

2 What is the *positive* which you assign to each of the following comparatives; *further, nether, utter, former, latter?*

3. Parse fully the following lines:—

> As late each flower that sweetest blows
> I plucked, the garden's pride,
> Within the petals of a rose
> A sleeping love I spied.

N.B.—This third question must be taken.

*Geography.*

1. Draw a full map of Cumberland, Westmoreland, and Lancashire.

2. Describe, as exactly as you can, the situation and character of Liverpool, Chester, Hull, Bristol, Oxford, Cambridge, and Southampton.

N.B.—*Do not merely give the place where each town stands, but say something of the character of the country round it, &c., &c.*

3. Name the chief lakes of Scotland and Ireland, and describe their situations and the character of the surrounding country. If you have learnt any part of the "Lady of the Lake," quote lines in illustration of the scenery of Loch Katrine.

*Composition.*

Write from memory the substance of the passage read to you by the inspector.

## END OF SECOND YEAR.

Three hours and a half allowed.

*Arithmetic.*

MALES.

1. What fraction of a mile is $\frac{2}{7}$ of $\frac{3}{4}$ of a mile + $\frac{5}{6}$ of $\frac{8}{5}$ of $2\frac{1}{2}$ furlongs + $\frac{3}{7}$ of 4 furlongs + $18\frac{3}{4}$ poles?

2. A farmer went to market with £$2\frac{3}{8}$ in his pocket. He received for wheat sold £$27\frac{5}{12}$; for barley, £$37\frac{7}{16}$; for oats, £$17\frac{3}{8}$; for poultry, $18\frac{3}{8}$s.; for eggs, $3\frac{5}{8}$s. How much did he bring home?

3. A merchant owns $\frac{4}{9}$ of a ship worth £3,000 and its cargo worth £27,000. He purchases another person's share, which is $\frac{1}{3}$ of $\frac{3}{8}$ of it. What part of it has he now, and what is its value?

4. Find by decimals (to three places) how often £1 19s. $11\frac{3}{4}$d. is contained in £173 18s. $6\frac{1}{2}$d.

FEMALES.

1. The first, third, and fourth terms of a proportion are 3 cwt. 14 lbs., £1 7s. 1d. and £5 1s. 10d. respectively. Find the second terms.

2. If the wages of 13 men for $7\frac{1}{2}$ days amount to £13 7s. $0\frac{1}{2}$d., how many men ought to work for 4 weeks £173 8s.?

3. If $\frac{3}{5}$ yards of ribbon cost $3\frac{1}{2}$d., what will be the cost of $6\frac{1}{2}$ pieces, each containing $185\frac{1}{2}$ ells?

4. If 24 lbs. of wool make 115 yards of cloth 1 yard wide, how much cloth $1\frac{1}{4}$ yards wide ought 12 oz. to make.

*Grammar.*

1. What is a preposition? also, show in short sentences, that each of the prepositions *by*, *of*, and *with* is used in more than one sense.

## END OF FOURTH YEAR.

Three and a half hours allowed.

*Arithmetic.*

MALES.

1. A customer lodged £175 in the bank at $4\frac{1}{2}$ per cent. per annum simple interest. What sum ought he to be able to draw out again at the end of 6 years and 10 months?

2. A man sold a quantity of snuff for £50, and by so doing lost $33\frac{1}{3}$ per cent. What sum should he have sold it for to get $2\frac{11}{40}$ times what he had given for it?

3. A tradesman starts with a capital of £6,500, and makes an annual profit of $12\frac{1}{2}$ per cent. At what rate do his annual personal expenses increase if his capital only increases £100 a year, and what are his personal expenses the first year?

4. What is the difference between paying £1,200 by four quarterly instalments of £300, each instalment after payment bearing interest at 6 per cent. per annum, and by two half-yearly payments of £600, each instalment bearing interest at $6\frac{1}{2}$ per cent.

FEMALES.

1. What number added to the sum of ·0007 + 2·4 + ·05 + 3·0436 + ·047 will make an integer?

2. Express the difference between $\frac{3}{4}$ pk., and ·0625 of a bushel, as the decimal of a quarter.

3. If 40 men can reap 400·6 ac. in 12·75 days, how many acres ought 30 men to reap in 3·4 days?

4. A man having given $\frac{3}{8}$ of the money in his purse for a sheep, and ·375 of the remainder for a horse, had 1·6875 still left. What sum had he at first?

*Grammar.*

1. There was once a young shepherd, who wished to marry, and knew three sisters; but *as* each one was *as* pretty *as* the *others* he was doubtful *which* to prefer.

Analyse the foregoing passage, and parse the words which are in italics.

2. *Latum* means in Latin "brought" or "carried." Explain from the derivation the following words:—*Ablative, collate, dilate, elated, illative, relative, correlative, superlative, translation.*

*Geography.*

1. Draw a full map of the Caspian Sea.

2. Give a short account of the islands on the east and south-east of Asia, describing generally the character of the inhabitants of each.

3. Give notes of a lesson to a young class on "a map of the Eastern Hemisphere," explaining the shape of it, the lines which cross it, &c., and giving general ideas about the reason of the differences of climate in different countries according to their distance from the equator.

## END OF FOURTH YEAR (SECOND PAPER).

One hour allowed for Females.

Two hours and a half allowed for Males.

*History.*

1. Tell how the Houses of York and Lancaster were united, and sketch the character of Henry VII.'s queen?

2. What do you know about Princess Elizabeth, daughter of James I., and about her descendants?

3. To what causes would you attribute the prosperity of the United Kingdom?

*Composition.*

Write from memory the substance of the passage read to you by the Inspector.

*Euclid.*

1. The opposite sides and angles of a parallelogram are equal to one another, and the diameter bisects the parellelogram—that is, divides it into two equal parts.

2. If the three sides of a triangle be produced, the sum of the exterior angles is equal to four right angles.

## END OF FIFTH YEAR.

Three hours and a half allowed.

*Arithmetic.*

1. How much higher will the terminus of a railroad 280 miles long be than its starting point, if for ·25 of its length the line ascends 1 foot in 90, and for the last ·1 of its length descends 1 foot in 55, the remainder being level.

2. At what per centage, compound interest, would 750 amount in two years to £826 17s. 6d?

3. A man makes his will that the *first four* legatees are to be paid in full before anything is given to the others. He bequeaths to A £3,750, to B £3,525, to C £3,280, to D £2,000, to E £1,895, to F £1,750, to G £1,668, to H £1,745, to K £1,475, and to L £1,067. The whole estate turns out to be worth £19,575. How should the money be distributed.

4. What is the present value of £195,585 due one year nine months hence—discount at 6 per cent. per annum?

5. Took money out of a bank giving $2\frac{1}{2}$ per cent., and bought five £20 shares bearing interest at $8\frac{1}{2}$ per cent. the share to be paid up in six equal instalments. I at once paid up five instalments, and at the end of a year and a-half the property having increased $17\frac{1}{2}$ per cent. in value, I sold my shares. What did I gain by the whole transaction.

*Grammar.*

1.

> Alas! how light a cause may move
> Dissension between hearts that *love;*
> Hearts *that* the world in vain had tried
> And sorrow *but* more closely *tied,*
> That stood the storm when waves were rough,
> Will yet in sunny hour fall off.

Analyse the above lines and parse the words which are in italics.

2. From what language are the greatest number of English words derived?

*Composition.*

Write a short essay on *Punctuality* in the language you would use if you were giving a lesson to a first class.

2. Parse the following:—

> "Old yew, which graspest at the stones
> That name the underlying dead,
> Thy fibres met the dreamless head;
> Thy roots are wrapped about the bones."

*Geography.*

1. Draw a map of the coast line from Cape Matapan to the Dardanelles.

2. Give notes of a lesson on "lakes" under these heads:—*a.* How lakes are formed. *b.* Character of the scenery usually found round them. *c.* Illustrations from England, Scotland, Ireland, Switzerland, and Italy.

3. Where and what are Ajaccio, Amiens, Bayonne, St. Bernard, Cherbourg, Dordogne, Havre, Isyere, Macon, Metz, Nice, Oleron, Sèvres, Ushant? *Say something about at least six of the above, and more if you have time.*

*History.*

1. Give the dates of the following events:—*a.* The building of Hadrian's wall. *b.* The building of Antonine's wall. *c.* Departure of the Romans from Britain.

2. Write down a list of English sovereigns from William I. to Henry II. with dates.

3. Tell when our Queen ascended the throne, mention her Majesty's parentage and relationship to the three proceding sovereigns.

*Composition.*

Write from memory the substance of the passage read to you by the inspector.

## END OF THIRD YEAR.

Three hours and a half allowed.

*Arithmetic.*

MALES.

1. I invested £730 on 25th March, and on the 29th September following it amounted to £777. What was the rate of interest per cent. per annum?

2. If in a school of 360 children 27 play truant and 63 are sick, what per centage of non-attendance is due to truancy and to sickness respectively?

3. In what time will any sum of money treble itself at $2\frac{1}{2}$ per cent. and at $12\frac{1}{2}$ per cent. per annum, simple interest?

4. If the proportion of nitrogen in the air is 79 per cent., and of oxygen 20 per cent., what quantity of nitrogen and oxygen respectively will there be in an apartment containing 908,600 gallons of air?

# The child teacher

The 1870 Act brought a rapid expansion in the number of pupil-teachers but later in the century numbers dropped, especially among boys, as other jobs opened up. Only a minority went to training colleges, which were all voluntary. By 1900 43 colleges were training just over 1,000 students. The small band of trained certificated teachers were in danger of being swamped by a growing flood of untrained assistant teachers, and the Union's fears about 'dilution' were proving well-founded.

Some developments were encouraging, however. Central classes for pupil-teachers had been started in London and had become popular elsewhere. Even more significant was the appearance of day training centres following the Cross Commission in 1889. Attached to several of the new universities as well as Oxford and Cambridge, they gave teachers in training the opportunity to be taught by university lecturers and to read for a degree. Many training colleges also allowed students to stay an extra year to read for an external degree.

This was the first step away from the closed system of elementary school teaching. The NUT supported the ideal of the integration of pupil-teacher training with secondary schools and training colleges with universities, and envisaged a united profession. But opposition came from secondary teachers who wanted to retain their separate identity.

1. How many teachers today would care to tackle this examination of pupil-teachers? They were examined and certificated by the Inspector.

2. An indenture setting out the terms of service of a pupil-teacher.

3. A student being examined in her classroom technique at Bishop Otter College, in Chichester. Practically all training colleges before 1900 were run by the Church of England.

4. The oldest training college in England and one of the few which did not impose a religious test on applicants was the Borough Road Training College. It had evolved from the Borough Road School and in 1890 it moved to new quarters in Isleworth, where it is still going strong. This common room, bare though it is to modern eyes, was a great improvement on earlier conditions.

2

4

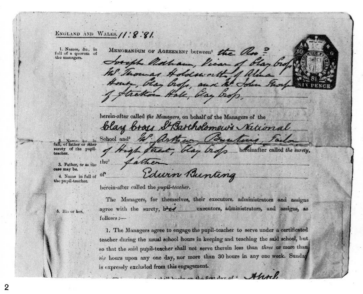

3

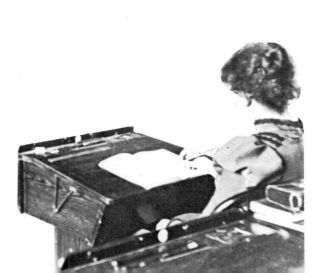

# Learning and leisure for the rich

1

Secondary education – the term came into general use at the end of the century – was not originally intended for elementary scholars and was held to be outside the responsibility of the state. But in various ways secondary education did develop. The teaching of 'specific' subjects, usually scientific, became centralised and developed into higher grade Board schools, mainly in northern towns.

The Science and Art Department at Kensington gave grants to all kinds of schools for teaching scientific and technical subjects. County Councils were able to use 'whisky money' (compensation for redundant publicans – that Victorian morality would not allow to go to its rightful recipients), either for paying policemen's pensions or improving technical education and many used it for the latter purpose. All this meant haphazard development with overlapping authorities, and emphasis on narrow technical training. In 1900 the Cockerton judgment which denied the right of School Boards to supply higher grade education meant that the Government had to decide on a policy for secondary education.

1. Boating at Eton under Windsor Castle. The second half of the 19th century saw the establishment of the public school system as we know it. Thomas Arnold was only one of a generation of reforming headmasters who laid emphasis on character-building and games and broadened the curriculum. Meanwhile the old endowed grammar schools excluded local foundationers and became fee-paying schools for the middle-classes. An elitist secondary education evolved, free of all government control.

2. The best of the science schools attracted graduate scientists as teachers. It was clear that they were seeking for the same relationship with the new universities that the grammar and public schools had with the old.

3. The Science and Art Department in Kensington had been created after the 1851 Exhibition with the idea of encouraging scientific developments. It was technically under the supervision of the Vice-President of the Committee of Council, like the Education Department, but it was a case of the right hand not knowing what the left hand was doing.

4. The masses don't want higher education, said Punch. But it was scarcely true. A trend towards staying on at school after 12 was growing, and 'night schools', working men's institutes and every sort of college open to ordinary people were enthusiastically attended.

# Mechanics for the poor

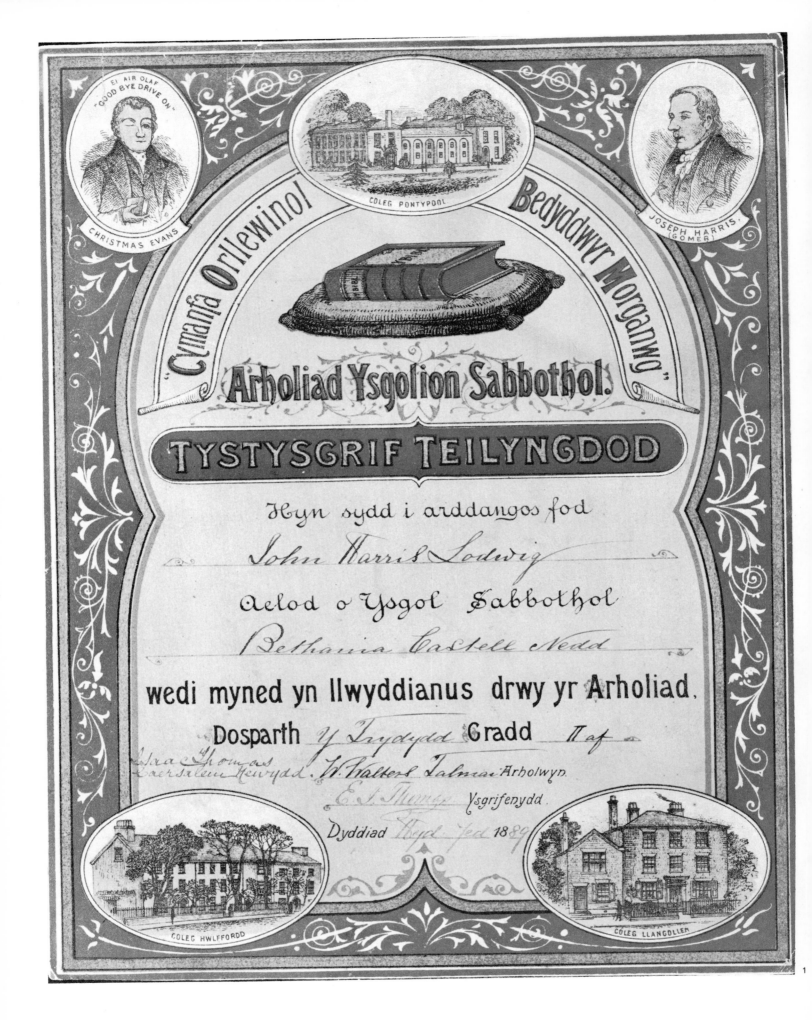

1.  Sunday schools were a vital element in Welsh society from the 18th century onwards. Setting out to teach young and old to read the Bible, they were instrumental in the spread of Calvinist Methodism through North and South Wales. Before any formal education had developed, they helped to spread literacy and to preserve Welsh as a written language. This certificate was presented to a West Glamorgan scholar in 1889. Joseph Harris and Christmas Evans were famous preachers – 'Goodbye, drive on' were the latter's dying words.

# Wales the same but different

The system of state education, begun in 1870, applied equally to England and Wales, but there have always been distinguishing features to schooling in the Principality. Even more than in England, the early history of elementary education was determined by religious controversy between Church and Dissent, bound up as it was with differences in class, culture, and language. In a poor country, education was highly prized, and only a genuine popular demand can explain the precocious development of secondary education after the 1889 Intermediate Act. In the 20th century, Wales has always had a high proportion of its children going on to secondary school, and of these a large number have become teachers. The long tradition of Welsh teaching makes it highly appropriate that Welsh members succeeded in forestalling a move in 1889 to rename the National Union of Elementary Teachers the National Union of English Teachers. The National Union of Teachers, in name at least, is a Welsh creation.

2. In 1907, a Welsh Department of the Board of Education was established to satisfy, in part at least, the demand for Welsh autonomy in educational matters. Its first team, pictured here, was led by Owen M. Edwards, Chief Inspector, who is seated second from the left. His aim was to allow Welsh schools to develop along their own lines as much as possible, and under his guidance the place of Welsh in the curriculum was assured. He had considerable faith in the ability of teachers to decide what they should teach and trusted the NUT to make professional decisions.

3. Ardwyn Grammar School in Aberystwyth, founded in 1896. By 1907 there were 96 new intermediate schools built under the 1889 Intermediate Act, which applied to Wales alone. Under the Act, the newly formed County Councils were allowed to finance Secondary Schools, and its successful operation influenced the drafting of the 1902 Education Act, which set up local education authorities.

# The 1902 Act comes to the rescue of church schools

By the end of the century, the need for a radical redefinition of the 1870 Act had become imperative. The main problems were the parlous financial position of the voluntary schools, the untidy growth of secondary education and the future of the School Boards. In 1900, the Tories were returned with a massive majority, and the Education Bill of 1902 proposed rate aid to voluntary schools and the replacement of School Boards by County and County Borough Councils which had been created in 1888.

One of a series of handbills setting out objections to the Bill.

A massive Free Church demonstration against rate aid for voluntary schools.

Education Bill Series—IV.

## Why the Education Bill must be opposed.

Because it destroys the present system of undenominational teaching in Board Schools.

Clause 27 of the Bill destroys THE COWPER TEMPLE CLAUSE of the Act of 1870 which provided that in no Board School should there be allowed to teach its dogmas, if it can get hold of a "reasonable" number of parents to ask that their children may receive such instruction.

Lord Salisbury, last year, told the Church Party that what they had to do was "TO CAPTURE THE BOARD SCHOOLS." This Clause 27 is put in the Bill to enable this to be done.

The parents, whose wishes alone have to be considered in this matter of religious instruction, have never shown any dissatisfaction with the present undenominational system which has worked well for the last quarter of a century.

Not only is its destruction not asked for by the parents, but it is HIGHLY DISTASTEFUL TO THE TEACHERS, who have already strongly protested against it.

At present, though denominationalism can not be taught, religious instruction is reverently and regularly given in our Board Schools. Why should this system be destroyed to allow one particular religious body to "Capture the Schools"?

44

# The birth of the modern system

For the NUT the Balfour-Morant Act of 1902 was a moment of truth. It brought teachers face to face with the decay of the voluntary schools, and all the emotive reactions summed up in the nonconformist slogan about 'putting Rome on the rates'; it brought them up against the question of how best to advance the education of the working class, indeed to a decision on the nature of education itself; and, by limiting entry to the profession to the products of the new 'secondary' system, it presented them with a conflict between their idealism for the education of all children, and their desire to enhance their own occupational status.

What was the Act of 1902? It was presented as a Bill by A. J. Balfour, who became the Conservative Prime Minister during the debates; it was largely inspired by Robert Morant, previously the educational adviser to the King of Siam, whose ambitious and conspiratorial character was recruited as permanent secretary of the new Government Board of Education, set up in 1899. The first of three great Education Acts to be produced by a Britain at war, it was also the first comprehensive education Bill to reach the Statute Book. It abolished the School Boards and turned the counties and county boroughs into education authorities (though smaller authorities were allowed power over elementary schools); it clearly distinguished between elementary and secondary schools (though on a class basis as much as on an educational one) and allowed authorities to spend up to a 2d rate on secondary education; it granted rate support for voluntary schools, although leaving the voluntary bodies a clear majority on the boards of managers; and it laid the basis for a scholarship system for potential elementary teachers at secondary schools, a vast expansion in teacher training colleges, and the demise of the pupil-teacher system.

Introducing his Bill, Mr Balfour deployed a number of arguments. He blamed the 1870 Act for embarrassing the voluntary schools, and for creating a system of fiscally irresponsible School Boards which handed over rate demands to the local authorities which the latter were then bound to pay. There was no organisation for voluntary schools, *'there was no sufficient provision for the education of the great staff of teachers needed for our national schools'*, and there was no rational connection between primary, secondary and university education. It was Parliament's duty to remedy *'the insufficiency of the supply of secondary education'*, to end the competition between county and borough councils (responsible for technical education under the 1889 Act) and the School Boards in the secondary field, and to sort

Sir John Gorst

Sir Robert Morant

A. J. Balfour

out the education of teachers.

'Any child who wishes to become a teacher gets made a pupil-teacher, and when he has reached that status half his time goes to teaching and the other half . . . to learning . . . What is the result? . . . I find that 36 per cent . . . have never got through the examination for the certificate, and that 55 per cent of the existing teachers have never been to a training college of any sort', he said. He argued that the country was not getting proper value for the £18m spent annually on elementary education while, in an appeal to educationalists, he claimed that his proposals would improve a situation which was alarming many leaders of opinion: that Britain was falling 'behind all its Continental and American rivals in the matter of education'.

The factors which led to a general rearrangement of the educational system in 1902 were varied, and somewhat contradictory. A leading one, to a Conservative Government, was naturally the desperate plight of the Anglican voluntary schools. In 1897, following the failure of an Education Act that would have assisted voluntary schools and curbed the School Boards, the Conservative Government gave a free handout of over £600,000 to the necessitous voluntary schools. By 1902, although these schools were still at a disadvantage, the skilful tactics of Sir John Gorst, the Conservative Education Minister had meant that they were already substantially supported by public funds; the exchequer was bearing 77 per cent of the cost, subscriptions produced 14 per cent, and other sources of revenue the remaining 9 per cent. To nonconformists, who reckoned that up to half the children in Anglican voluntary schools were in fact theirs, and to the labour movement, this public support without popular control or nonsectarian religion was a continuing irritation.

But if the 1902 Act was a Conservative answer to the problem of hard pressed Anglican elementary schools, it was also a

solution, backed by the Fabians, for the confusion over schooling for teenagers. Here, piecemeal and under the stimulus of differing agencies, a great expansion was taking place. In the elementary schools by the 90s there was a general trend towards staying on beyond the age of 12; it was officially estimated in 1893-4 that three-quarters of all children aged 12 to 13 'of the class usually found in public elementary schools' were still on the register; by 1894-5 there were over 50,000 youngsters over 14 who were still at school.

Nurturing this early demonstration of a recurring phenomenon – voluntary staying on – were the large School Boards in particular and their elementary teachers. Much of the demand was met by growing 'higher tops' to the conventional elementary schools, classes which allowed both the pupils and the teachers to develop more interesting work. But in the 80s and 90s, particularly in the north of England, a number of 'higher grade schools', often called central schools, were set up by the Boards. Their special forte was science, technology and language teaching. The Royal Commission on Technical Instruction, which reported in 1884 when worries about the lag of British industry were already growing, found the work of these pioneer schools to be praiseworthy. 'This higher grade school represents a new educational movement from below, and a demand from new classes of the population for secondary education which has sprung up in a few years', commented an assistant commissioner to the Bryce Commission in 1895.

However the Cross Commission in the previous decade had expressed hostility to the higher grade schools, largely because they were seen as a threat to the middle and upper classes, and the Bryce Commission, by recommending that there should be a distinct pattern of secondary education which counties and county boroughs should provide, helped to undermine both this growth and the

School Boards. One of the main supports for the higher grade schools and the higher tops had been the special grants available from the Science and Art Department in South Kensington which had been earmarked for 'the industrial classes'. But in the late 90s, as part of the strategy developed by Sir John Gorst and Robert Morant to limit the Boards and the upward movement of the elementary

The Union's strike headquarters at West Ham. The poster announcing that qualified teachers were wanted outside West Ham illustrates a trump card played by the NUT.

system, Science and Art grants had to be paid via counties and county boroughs.

Since 1889 the counties and county boroughs had become responsible for higher technical education and since the following year, in an inspiring example of how Victorian administrators could distil virtue out of vice, some three-quarters of a million pounds of 'whisky money' (resulting from the Local Taxation (Customs and Excise) Act) became available to these authorities annually. Though the first charge of 'whisky money' was to pay for pensions for policemen it was also designed to forward technical education; in practice substantial sums were paid over for the rescue of endowed schools, especially the ancient but unimproved grammar schools, and they played a crucial part in restoring their fortunes. This mutual support between the county authorities and the grammar schools helps to explain the direction of policy for secondary education after 1902 when the former won sole responsibility.

The revival of that somnolent group of grammar schools which had not sailed away to become acknowledged public schools may well date from the activities of the Endowed Schools Commission, which overhauled

charters and hinted that some curricula were in need of revision in the 1870s. But in the late 19th century there was much fear in these schools that the higher grade schools, with their modern outlook and firm rate support, were underselling them. Grammar school teachers felt the need to organise and in 1890 the Headmasters Association was formed to fight for a genuine secondary school system; it fought the higher grade schools and inevitably came into conflict with the NUT. (The class difference in the two types of school was neatly shown by a return in 1897 which recorded that 91·2 per cent of higher grade school pupils came from elementary schools, compared with 48·9 per cent of grammar school pupils; over a third of the higher grade group were the children of manual workers while only 6·8 per cent of the grammar children were.)

Long before the 1902 Act, or the significant Liberal amending Act of 1907 which required rate aided secondary schools to offer 25 per cent of free places to the local authority, some counties were already obtaining scholarship places at grammar schools. One of the keenest to do so was Sidney Webb, who as chairman of the London County Council's technical education board envisaged an educational 'ladder' linking the elementary school to the university. He talked about his 'capacity catching machine' – not such a different concept from the 'pool of ability' theory that informed the Robbins Report in the 1960s – and the resultant competition among elementary London schoolchildren for grammar places makes it possible to regard Webb as one of the fathers of the eleven plus. But this elitist view, to which he converted the Fabian Society, was always anathema in broader reaches of the labour movement.

The final clearing of the ground for the 1902 Act was achieved in 1899 and 1900 by adroit moves by Gorst and Morant. Morant conceived that the swelling extension of School Board activities might have no legal basis and in June, 1899, with certain encouragement from the Government and officers of the London County Council, the North London School of Art, complaining of competition from evening classes run by the London School Board brought a case against it. Named after Cockerton, the district auditor who disallowed spending from the rates by the School Board on science and art schools or classes, the final judgment on appeal stated that a School Board had no right to spend any portion of the school fund on education that came under the Science and Art Department.

Meantime, before the appeal was finally settled, the Board of Education had shown its hand by a Minute on higher education which severely circumscribed the growth of higher grade schools and 'higher tops'. First a strict upper age limit of 15 was imposed on elementary schools; second only a selection of the existing higher grade schools would be recognised by the Board as 'higher elementary' schools; third, these would be confined to a narrow range of pupils, subjects and equipment; fourth, they should not contain pupils who 'ought to have gone' to endowed secondary schools; and fifth, they would have to steer a middle line in curriculum and

equipment between normal elementary schools and other secondary schools. In retrospect this Minute looks like a charter for secondary modern schools.

What then were the secondary schools for which the 1902 Act was to give such an enormous stimulus? Above all, were they 'secondary' in the mid 20th century idiom, separated from schools for younger children by age of entry, or were they 'secondary' because they offered a different but parallel instruction to 'elementary' schools? There was a confusion here from the start but the fact that the second attitude had as strong an influence in the administration of the Act as the first helps to explain the lasting association of grammar schools, the paragons of 1902, with the idea of an exclusive middle class education. The 1904 regulations for secondary schools laid stress on a general education for the 12–16 age group as being the hallmark of such a school, though it accepted that entry could occur at eight or even earlier.

The administrative action of the Board, in the critical years before 1906 when the Liberals were returned to office, helped to shore up secondary schools as a system of class education from which working class children were broadly excluded. It insisted on a minimum fee of £3 a year – in 1907 the president of the NUT observed that 607 schools were charging more than £3 and that only four were completely free – and, in cooperation with the new local authorities, it ensured that only a trivial number of the higher grade schools were approved as 'higher elementary' schools. (Although the grammar schools were the prototypes of the new system of secondary education it is interesting that the 1904 regulations already held the germ of that distinction between grammar and other secondary schools which would be the next line of defence for elitists when popular demand for a post elementary education became too strong: 'Secondary schools are of different types, suited to the different requirements of the scholars, to their place in the social organisation, and to the means of the parents and the age at which the regular education of the scholars is obliged to stop short, as well as to the occupations and opportunities of development to which they may or should look forward in later life'.)

This indicates what a difficult challenge the 1902 scheme for secondary schooling presented to the elementary teachers. The problem was compounded because it was intimately bound up with their status and their own training. From one angle the demand for a coordinated system of secondary schools was a tribute to their success in the elementary schools; but if the result was to impose a network of publicly subsidised schools on top of theirs, in which they were kept from teaching, it brought them no benefit. They also had a direct stake in the secondary field in the pupil-teacher centres that had grown up to provide some further education for intending teachers; in the event many were converted into orthodox secondary schools.

Status had been a sore point with the elementary teachers ever since the profession had been brought into being in the 1840s. They had been the butt of resentment from members of the old middle class – there were jokes about their 'over education' – and they had the insecure feeling of not knowing quite where they were in class-conscious Victorian England. By the turn of the century this insecurity was probably diminished, thanks in part to the strength and bargaining power

He had to be different! A class of infants in 1908 modelling a bird's nest. Their efforts appear somewhat repetitive today, but it was a real advance on earlier methods.

of the union. With figures like James Yoxall and T. J. Macnamara in the eye of the general public there could be little doubt of the calibre of the leading teachers.

Nevertheless they still felt shortcomings in their own level of education. 'The organised thousands of the National Union of Teachers have aspirations toward that high intellectual plane which has come to be embodied in one word – "culture", said the president of the Union, James Blacker, in 1901. In this, and in their yearning for the respectability of the profession, they fell in with the desires of establishment educationalists since Matthew Arnold who had seen education as an instrument for humanising, and taming, the working classes. But by accepting a cut in the new humanist middle class secondary education were they not also denigrating the developing technical and other education of their own higher grade schools? (Round the turn of the century, it must be remembered, British industrialists were bewailing the relatively poor technical training the majority of youngsters had had, and offices were even importing German clerks.)

Swirling about the 1902 Act then were controversies which in differing forms would persist long into the twentieth century. They turned on the meaning of education, in almost the same way as one may argue now about the meaning of higher education as applied to both Oxford and a polytechnic. They tied in with attitudes to the training of teachers – for while the elementary teachers laughed at the untrained teachers in grammar

schools, the latter sneered at the former's illiberal education. They concerned the best way to achieve an educational advance in the general population; given prevailing social attitudes and willingness to pay, was it better to put middle class schooling on a sound footing for the first time and then widen the access of other children, or should there be continuous piecemeal progress for all children? The teachers were being offered half a loaf or no bread, a choice that would become increasingly familiar.

The storm over the 1902 Act can scarcely be imagined now. Piloted by the incoming Prime Minister it was debated in the Commons for 57 days, the debates spanning the conclusion of peace in the Boer War, and the 'pro Boer', David Lloyd George used his considerable oratorical powers to castigate the Bill as a means of 'riveting the clerical yoke on thousands of parishes in England'. (His threat of passive resistance was in fact carried out by a subsequent refusal of some Welsh Nonconformists to pay that part of their rates which they calculated would go to Anglican schools.) The Nonconformists held monster rallies, Labour speakers addressed huge meetings, and a Radical Baptist captured a traditional Conservative constituency in Leeds after fighting a by-election entirely on the education issue.

The Union, with its MP representatives, was in the thick of the fight. On the issue that bulked largest at the time, the rate aid to church schools, the union, with its roots in the 1870 compromise, took a commonsense attitude. Its stand was that for the sake of the children and the teachers the country could not afford to go on permitting the standards in half its schools to be so markedly inferior to the rest; for this it was bitterly attacked by the extreme nonconformists. Over the abolition of the School Boards, some of which had served teachers so well, the union had regrets. It would have preferred an ad hoc authority, over which it could gain more influence, but it recognised the administrative simplicity of a bigger all-in authority. Along with the Liberals and the Labour movement it was determined that a majority of members of the education committees should be

answerable to the electorate; it was James Yoxall, during the report stage of the Bill, who moved a successful amendment that, except in the case of a county council, the committees should contain a majority of members who were also members of the local council.

The Union helped to get the Bill amended so that the age for possible attendances at day schools was raised from 15 to 16 and the rate limit of 2d in the £ for higher education was removed for county boroughs – a concession which gave crucial aid to the expansion of civic secondary schools. The Union got promises of an end to extraneous duties, of more help for the training of non-Anglicans who wished to be teachers, and had a clause inserted in the Bill which enabled local authorities to spend money on the training of teachers. Perhaps of most direct satisfaction, and the product of carefully planned lobbying, was the passage of an amendment protecting teachers in voluntary schools. This required that 'the consent of the Authority shall also be required to the dismissal of a teacher unless the dismissal be on grounds connected with the giving of religious instruction in the school'; this was a major safeguard and put an end to the tyranny of rural parsons and others.

The Union, which had helped to kill the first education Bill of the Conservatives in 1896 when it became obvious that it involved religious tests on Board school teachers, was moderately happy with the 1902 Act by the time it was passed. In their pleasure at a solution to the difficulties of the voluntary schools, and their delight at the appearance of a unified educational structure, the teachers seem to have underrated the elitist and hostile attitude that animated Morant's Board. While the Union looked forward to a unified teaching profession for all types of school and no distinctions between the education of a middle- and working-class child – an outlook which brought it the help of the organised Labour movement – the actions of the Board and the new authorities made it very difficult for elementary teachers to teach in secondary schools, or for working class children to learn in them. (At least until the chink opened by the 1907 free place requirement.)

However the Union saw what was happening quickly enough afterwards, and accused the Board of 'thwarting and hindering the higher educational interests of the children of the working classes'! It inveighed against the narrowing of the curricula in the higher elementary schools, and the Board's encouragement of fees in the secondary schools. (Not the least in the factors making for disillusionment was the snobbery that working class scholarship holders and intending teachers came up against in the grammar schools.) But Morant had done his work well – though like Forster in an earlier generation he would have been shattered by the expense to which his proposals gave rise – and within five years the union had abandoned all hopes for the higher elementary schools, and for the professional and technical education to which they had pointed. It was forced to press for an extension of scholarships in grammar schools, and an end to the fees.

# The turn of the century

In 1899, the educational functions of the central government were unified in the Board of Education under a single Minister, the President. The 1902 Act achieved the same sort of rationalisation at local level. For the first time, elementary and higher education were brought together under the control of the new local education authorities.

With 30 odd years of experience behind it, the Union was in a strong position to bargain with the untried local authorities. It drew up a union scale for certificated teachers and developed sophisticated techniques for dealing with recalcitrant authorities. But the policy of strict delimitation between elementary and secondary schools, originating from the Board of Education, bore harshly on Union members. Paradoxically, the secondary teachers themselves felt the bureaucratic rein tighten and a rapprochement took place between the two groups. A Teacher's Register in 1912 embracing elementary and secondary teachers was a first step towards a united profession. The Union began to wield greater influence at national and local level than ever before.

1. Drill was a prominent feature of the curriculum at the turn of the century.

# Union fights selection for grammar schools

'Secondary education for all' had been a Union ideal from 1870. Their hopes that the 1902 Act might go some way towards realising it were not fulfilled. Under Sir Robert Morant as Permanent Secretary, the Board pursued a policy of confining elementary education within clear limits and building up a co-ordinated system of secondary education for an elite in the grammar school tradition. Scholarships formed the only link between elementary and secondary schools. The NUT accused the Board of organising a 'system of secondary education for the middle-class apart.' In effect, a three-tier system had come into being: Independent public and grammar schools; new local authority day grammar schools, largely fee-paying and taking children from 7 or 8; and free elementary schools.

The Union was forced to devote its energies to pressing for more scholarships and more grammar schools. In 1907, all secondary schools receiving grants were compelled to provide free places for 25 per cent of their annual entry, and 11 plus became gradually accepted as the age when elementary pupils should sit the scholarship examinations. As Tawney put it: 'the free place system made a break, if a small one, in the walls of educational exclusiveness.'

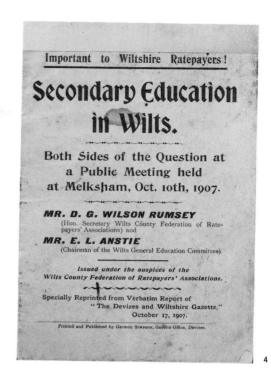

4

4. Financial considerations played a large part in deciding secondary school policy at national and local level. The Wiltshire ratepayers wanted fees at the county secondary schools to go up from 5 guineas to 7 guineas a year. Their spokesman, Mr. Rumsey, was not entirely disinterested; a private schoolmaster, he foresaw the 'gradual extinction of private schools' by unfair competition. The Wiltshire schools took in an unusually high proportion of ex-elementary pupils.

2

3

2. The headmaster reads a summary of the life of Captain Scott to pupils at the Hugh Myddelton School in London, which was shared by an elementary school and a central school. Central schools developed in London and the North as one of the types of 'lower secondary schools' recognised by the Board of Education for children who would 'earn their living in the lower ranks of commerce and industry.' Others were junior technical schools, trade schools,

and day and evening continuation schools. The Board made great efforts to ensure that they did not compete with the secondary schools proper.

3. A cartoon from *The Sun* in 1895 depicts the 'capacity-catching' system pioneered in London by Sydney Webb. It strongly influenced the developments of national policy after 1902. Webb succeeded in detaching the Fabians

from the main body of the Labour movement to support Tory policy on secondary schools. 'Free-placers' were mainly from the lower middle-class, and as a group they stayed on longer and achieved better results than the fee-paying pupils.

# The vision of education widens

The great majority of children attended only an elementary school and left at 12. The elementary school was treated as the poor relation of the secondary school; for example, a teacher-pupil ratio of 1 : 50 was allowed compared with 1 : 17 for the secondary school. But in the 1904 Code the Board outlined a remarkably liberal philosophy for elementary schools, and the pupils received a wider and better education than in the 19th century. The last vestiges of payment by results were swept away, leaving teachers with considerable freedom to decide what to teach in their classrooms.

1. 'An intelligent acquaintance with some of the facts and laws of nature' was specified in the Code. This science room was in the Aristotle Road School in London.

2. A laundry class at Tennyson Elementary School, which is now used by the Inner London Educational Television Service.

3. The manual training centre at Green Lane School in Bradford, one of the last schools to be built by the Bradford Board, and very well-equipped. The Code said that schools should 'encourage to the utmost the children's natural activities of hand and eye'.
   The present headmaster of Green Lane School is Harry Dawson, past president of the Union. It is one of the schools most concerned with immigrants.

4. A gallery class at a Bradford School. Teachers still had to cope with overcrowded conditions.

5. A lesson in natural history at the Albion Street elementary school in London, now the Albion primary school. The design of schools had changed from the 19th century pattern of one long room divided by movable partitions to individual classrooms leading off a central hall. We are now moving back to the idea of open-space schools made up of flexible teaching areas.

6. These children certainly seemed happy at the Hugh Myddelton School. They were celebrating Empire Day in 1913.

# County secondary schools follow the grammar school tradition

The 1904 Regulations for Secondary Schools spelt out the distinction between elementary and secondary education and decided that the new state secondary schools should follow the path blazed by the grammar and public schools. They were to provide, for a minimum of four years, 'a complete graded course of instruction of wider scope and more advanced degree than that given in elementary schools'. The Regulations carefully laid down the proportion of timetable hours which were to be alloted to different groups of subjects, but this attempt to dictate to the schools was dropped in 1907. In secondary schools as in elementary schools, teachers were allowed to decide the contents of the curriculum within the limits of the Code.

Under the Code, county secondary schools provided an academic education based slightly in favour of literary studies and decidedly in favour of the few who would go on to university. Sixth form studies developed as the most typical and successful aspect. In 1917, the universities were recognised as the proper bodies to run external examinations for the schools and the School Certificate Examination was born.

1. The Honours Board at Latymer School, Hammersmith, shows that university entrance was the principal goal. Founded in 1624, Latymer was one of the independent grammar schools which accepted LEA aid in return for conforming to the Code and taking free pupils. In 1926, it was one of 250 aided schools which opted for a capitation grant direct from the Board and thus became a direct-grant school.

2. The art room in Strand School, at Elm Park in London. 'Drawing' was given special prominence in the 1904 Code but the emphasis was on technical proficiency rather than on artistic imagination. Before it became a secondary school for boys in 1913, Strand School had been a department of King's College, London. It is still a county grammar school for boys.

1

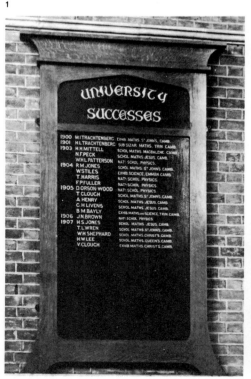

2

3

3. The importance attached to drill and physical training at this time owed much to the example of the Scandinavian countries. These girls, from Brondesbury and Kilburn High School, were taking part in a 'Swedish drill' competition. Teachers were brought from Sweden to spread the art.

4

5

6

4. A classroom at Fulham County Secondary School for girls, founded in 1905. Secondary education for girls had been pioneered by the Girls' Public Day School Trust in the second half of the 19th century and was expanded by the LEAs after 1902. The small class with individual desks is in sharp contrast to the over-crowded elementary schools.

5. Another girls' county secondary school at Clapham. Secondary schools were almost always single-sex, although there were few differences between the education provided for girls and boys. As this picture shows, segregation had its drawbacks.

6. The cadet battalion at Hackney Downs Secondary School in 1911, an endowed grammar school taken over by the LCC. Today it is in the process of becoming a comprehensive school.

# The pupil-teacher system declines

The Board's policy on teacher recruitment was to educate future teachers at secondary schools, a development distrusted by the Union. Pupil-teacher centres were gradually closed and local authorities paid bursaries to pupils at secondary schools who intended to train as teachers. The minimum age for pupil-teacher apprenticeships was raised to 16. The initial result was a drop in the number coming into the profession but it was an important move in the improvement of training. At first, student teachers were regarded as a separate and lowly group in secondary schools but they gradually became integrated and indeed were an important ingredient in the new sixth forms.

Twenty LEAs took advantage of their powers in the 1902 Act to build training colleges. An unfortunate result of the Board's policy of containing elementary education was that colleges were discouraged from operating three-year courses to include an external degree. The day-training colleges continued to offer four-year courses, and they also began to provide Diplomas in Education as professional training for graduates intending to teach in secondary schools.

**Examinations Board**

*of the*

**National Union of Teachers.**

**This is to Certify**

that *Joseph E. Dunn*

*having satisfied the Examiners*

*in the Elementary Stage*

*of Bookkeeping*

*is awarded this Certificate*

*of the First Class*

*General Secretary.*

*W. Hollingsworth*

*Secretary to Examinations Board*

*Date of issue* 1912
*Registered No.* 2425

1. A group picture taken in 1907 of all the staff and students of the University College of Nottingham, now the University of Nottingham. Among the student teachers at the day-training college was D. H. Lawrence (standing at the end of the second-back row, on the right). He had been a scholarship boy at Nottingham High School and had also served as a pupil-teacher at Eastwood. Leaving Nottingham with his teacher's certificate but no degree, he taught in Davidson's Road School in Croydon until he left to become a full-time writer. He was a member of the NUT in 1910.

2. A cookery class at the Elizabeth Gaskell College, Manchester. This college was one of the earliest to train specialist teachers. It was begun in 1880 as a training school for cookery and laundrywork and was taken over by the Manchester Education Committee in 1906.

3. A certificate issued by the NUT Examinations Board. An early aim of the Union had been for the teaching profession to be recognised as a diploma-granting authority, and the Board was set up in 1895 as a first step towards it. At first it was mainly concerned with tutorial examinations for pupil-teachers, then with commercial and handicraft examinations for part-time students. Many overseas students used the facilities. It was wound up in 1936 when it became apparent that the growth of other examinations left little scope.

# Aftermath of the 1902 Act and the Great War

In the first decade of the new century the Board of Education, for good or ill, was overwhelmingly concerned with setting up a comprehensive network of secondary schools. From staffing, building and other points of view these schools were generously treated by comparison with the elementary schools, to the inevitable annoyance of teachers in the latter. Nevertheless the relative neglect by officials was not unhealthy as far as the educational work of the elementary schools was concerned; in this period, it seems, came some of the first stirrings of that vitality and initiative – a child centred approach even – which, built on by later generations of alert and skilful teachers, were to make British primary teaching of the Plowden era the envy of the world.

One of the prides of education at this time was the quality of work in infant schools. In 1895, to the shame of 1970, there were over 600,000 children of three and four in school, or nearly half the age group. The infants had scarcely been touched by the restrictions of payment by results and their teaching lent inspiration to the efforts of teachers of older children when they were able to stretch their imaginations more freely. Even before the turn of the century HMIs had been commenting favourably on developments for infants. 'All the good teachers have more or less adopted the kindergarten method', wrote one. 'There is a visible and decided advance in the teaching and bad styles are disappearing, such as counting on the fingers and unnatural sing song. The old time formal methods, abstract and verbal, have been discarded and superseded by the real practical, vivid and concrete', stated another. With singing, handwork, games and dancing, the infant classes at the turn of the century were surprisingly modern in outlook.

In the first two decades of this century this fresher approach seems gradually to have spread to the older elementary children. Sums were made to reproduce calculations that they would really have had to make, perhaps of annual wages or a weekly milk bill, rather than the Biblical computations that appeared in some Victorian textbooks. Practical subjects gathered pace too; in 1902 special grants were given for the first time for cookery, laundrywork, dairywork, household management, manual instruction, cottage gardening and even for cookery for boys, in the seaport towns. The code of 1902 also for the first time authorised educational visits, a valuable breakthrough for deprived urban children. By the Fisher Act of 1918 the suffocatingly punitive regimes engendered by payment by results – 19th century ads in *The Schoolmaster* used to stress that 'disciplinarians' were wanted – were beginning to give ground. But elementary teachers were still wrestling with large classes; in 1912 it was estimated that there was one teacher to 50 children, compared with one to 17 in secondary schools.

It must also be admitted that, while many elementary teachers felt the influence of Morant's Board was malign, it too must share the credit for the progress of elementary schools in these years. In the introduction to the 1904 Code, whose financial provisions helped to liberalise the schools, there appeared an encouraging and idealistic manifesto. 'The purpose of the Public Elementary School is to form and strengthen the character and to develop the intelligence of the children entrusted to it, and to make the best use of the school years available, in assisting both girls and boys, according to their different needs, to fit themselves, practically as well as intellectually, for the work of life', it began. Its conclusion looked forward to Plowden: 'In all these endeavours the School should enlist, as far as possible, the interest and cooperation of the parents and the home in an united effort to enable the children not merely to reach their full development as individuals, but also to become upright and useful members of the community in which they live, and worthy sons and daughters of the country to which they belong'.

At this period, too, the union with other working class bodies achieved a number of social gains of benefit to schoolchildren. In 1906, following the pioneering work of Margaret McMillan in Bradford and Deptford, and a major campaign by the TUC and Labour groups significantly supported by Sir John Gorst, Parliament passed an Act enabling local authorities to feed necessitous children. (The Boer War had glaringly exposed the physical deficiencies of urban volunteers.) In 1907 an Act was passed that allowed authorities to set up a medical inspection system for schools, though medical treatment was only permitted in 1912. In both these cases there were long struggles to obtain permissive legislation followed by local battles to get councils to act on it.

In 1911 a Bill by the Liberal Government to raise the leaving age from 12 to 13 and to abolish the surviving half-time system fell a casualty to the war over the House of

In 1911 a wave of strikes by pupils in elementary schools hit the headlines. It was triggered off by an incident in Llanelli, when pupils paraded the streets demanding shorter school hours and an end to corporal punishment. Further outbreaks occurred in Liverpool, London and Manchester.

*The Schoolmaster* had no hesitation in blaming the sensational press for spreading it. It is not too fanciful to see these minor incidents as part of the general social unrest in the years before 1914.

Lords; the Bill would have enabled children to choose between staying on until they were 14, and taking continuation classes until they were 16. These proposals lay dormant until they were revived by H. A. L. Fisher in 1917–18. In all the period between the Acts of 1902 and 1918 the union of course favoured an extended length of schooling, and lent its weight to the improvement of social conditions for children. (Even before local authorities would own any responsibility, teachers like the famous Mrs Burgwin, out of their own money and time, were giving food and clothing to the children who were suffering most.)

But the first years of the century cannot be understood except by reference to the extraordinary breakdown of confidence that occurred between the union and Morant's Board. Probably at no time since have relations between such a large group of teachers and the Government agency responsible for directing their efforts become so bitter. Morant, able man that he was, was also ruthless and arrogant in his personal dealings. The terms on which he was constructing secondary education, his policy of filling the Board and Inspectorate with public school and Oxbridge men, and his policy of restricting elementary education and designing it as inferior, led to a campaign against him personally by the union which finally drove him from the Permanent Secretaryship, along with his Minister, Walter Runciman, in 1911. In that year *The Schoolmaster* commented, 'We do not wish to gag civil servants . . . but some of them must learn to be more open minded, less haughtily prejudiced, more patient, more accessible to argument, less class conscious, and less cocksure than some of them have been'. Although the Union's victory could not lead to a secondary education for all overnight it was as significant in its way as the successful struggle against payment by results.

The years before the outbreak of the First World War were filled with growing industrial unrest – the House of Lords reform had almost revolutionary overtones – and the spirit of the times was reflected in the union. In 1907 the NUT published a pamphlet, *Higher Education and the People's Children* which was subtitled 'An Appeal to the People against the policy of the Secondary Schools' Branch of the Board of Education'. In rejecting the official 'Report of the Consultative Committee upon Higher Elementary Schools' – which deprecated existing higher elementary schools for 'too broad and too ambitious educational aims' and envisaged some narrow 'lower' secondary schooling for working class children – the general secretary, James Yoxall, called for a 'crusade' along with the leaders of the working classes. The Union should 'march to the conquest of a stronghold of class prejudice in the Secondary Branch of the Board of Education'. At this time the NUT was cooperating closely with the TUC; in 1905 the Congress had passed a resolution in ringing tones. 'This Congress condemns the educational policy of the government as laid down in the Act of 1902, and in all subsequently issued Minutes and Regulations and demands the formulation of an educational programme based upon the principle of equal opportunities for all', it stated.

Other issues between the teachers and the Board involved entry into and regulation of the profession. In July 1903 the Board issued new pupil-teacher regulations by which intending teachers should not be employed to teach in elementary schools until they were 16 or 17, so that they might have a better secondary education; when they did become pupil-teachers firm limits were imposed on their teaching so that they could continue taking lessons. The Board acknowledged that there would be a 'class problem' for the pupil-teachers in secondary schools, and in fact some schools made invidious distinctions between pupil-teachers and other pupils, even to the extent of providing separate playgrounds. But the new 'bursar' system encouraged by the Board resulted in a sharp fall in the number of entrants to the profession, largely because of the delay in wage earning and the strain on a working class family budget that was entailed.

The union opposed the death of the pupil-teachers and the pupil-teacher centres partly, perhaps, out of conservatism and partly because members feared that though the new recruits might be better educated they would be less good at teaching. A feature of secondary school teachers which they distrusted was being foisted on the elementary schools. At the same time, due to the expansion of training colleges, they also had periodic anxieties that the larger number of certificated teachers who might now be thrown on the market at one time were not getting jobs. After 1909 the Union was actually dissuading entrants to the profession and there were clashes with the Board over the size of the unemployment problem.

But the essential ambiguity over education for teaching which was to dog both the union and teacher education – ought teachers to have a general education or a professional training? – led to another fight with Morant's Board. Busy demarcating the colleges' work so that it would provide a profession at training alone, the Board's administrative action made it next to impossible for a trainee teacher to get a degree. Up till 1902 there had been an increasing stream of students who had read for university degrees at their college and the union had looked forward to a time when a degree would have been part of the usual equipment of a teacher; this, obviously, would have been a major contribution to unifying the profession of teaching in elementary and secondary schools. In this quarrel the Union joined forces with the Association of Training College Principals and Lecturers and although in 1911 the Board recognised training departments attached to universities which might prepare teachers for the elementary schools the substantive issue, a fair chance for all teachers to take a degree, would remain unfinished business into the 1960s.

On another matter, which would also leave a legacy into the 1960s, the Union was able to surmount mutual differences in a joint campaign against the Board. This was over a Teachers' Registration Council, ghostly ancestor to Mr Short's Teachers' General Council. Getting Parliament to enact that there should be a Council had been a success of the union in 1899. But instead of the single alphabetical list implied by the Act an Order in Council prescribed that there should be a double columned list, one for those who could teach in elementary schools, the second for those who had already taught in secondary schools. The NUT campaigned against this divisive 'caste' register, the

Hamilton House, which was opened as the Union's headquarters in 1913.

Board, which disliked the Act which had established it, ignored it. Fundless and friendless the Council was nearly wiped out by the Board in 1907 but a new alliance between the union and secondary teachers, including the HMA, fought for a revived Council on the basis of a single column register. In 1911 the teachers, combined at last, got Morant to accept a new Council, although it could not compel registration and was less powerful than was hoped.

Morant's downfall from the Board occurred in an unexpected fashion. It resulted from a press leak of a memorandum to HMIs which called their attention to the bad effects of appointing ill equipped and narrow minded people to be local authority inspectors. In principle, of course, it had always been the aim of teachers to open all inspectorial positions to promoted teachers and they were glad that many School Boards had done so. Many of these inspectors were subsequently taken over by the new local authorities and formed the target of what was to be known as the Holmes Morant Circular. But in practice there had been some friction between working teachers and just this type of local inspector; the inquiry that lead to the memorandum seems to have arisen out of a complaint by James Yoxall to Mr E. G. A. Holmes, the chief inspector for elementary schools, that certain local inspectors were trying to reimpose a vicious system of examinations.

However in the anti Morant atmosphere of 1911 the leaked memorandum became a banner which united several groups with the union in a sustained attack on the class prejudice and undemocratic composition of the Board's officials. The Conservatives, in opposition, used the issue to embarrass the Liberal Government. Members of the Liberal Party, uncomfortable about the reactionary policies of the Board, or angry at its unavenged destruction of the old School Boards, joined in the furore. Members of the Union and speakers from the civil service unions addressed a large meeting at the Albert Hall on May 13, 1911 at which demands were made for the general opening up of the higher civil service to talents from all parts of the population. Runciman, the President of the Board who told the Commons that there had never been such a circular, was forced out of office; Morant, who had been knighted in 1907, was transferred to work on Lloyd George's new insurance scheme in November.

Although the local authorities that were administering education after 1902 did not always do their job as the Union would have wished their arrival, more powerful than the School Boards or voluntary managers, provided the Union with a golden opportunity to improve teachers' salaries. This it eagerly took, by formulating a standard scale of salaries for certificated teachers in elementary schools, by paying the removal expenses of underpaid teachers in rural areas, and by striking, or threatening to strike, against recalcitrant authorities. The first teachers' strike had been in Portsmouth in 1896. In 1907 there was a major confrontation with West Ham Council in which the withdrawal of teachers from the schools was accompanied by an appeal to the West Ham public; the borough, which had been trying to cut teacher salaries, was made to come to terms.

In 1913, when a rising cost of living hit teachers and was causing unrest among manual workers, the NUT launched an agitation to get a national salary scale. It also joined other teacher bodies to seek earmarked grants to local authorities which could be devoted to the improvement of staffing ratios and the raising of salaries. In 1914 the union closed 60 schools in Herefordshire when the county refused to introduce a single scale for its teachers. It was a formidable demonstration of the union's power and caused some resentment. But after mediation by the Bishop of Hereford the county agreed to a satisfactory scale.

Immediately after the outbreak of the 1914 war the union halted its salaries campaign, which had obtained improvements in almost half the local authority areas. Throughout the war the union tried to maintain 'education as usual', though events made this scarcely possible. Over half the men teachers went into the forces – the resentments of some who returned would be capitalised to start the National Association of Schoolmasters on its stormy career – and in their place retired teachers, married women who had been teachers and even clergymen were pressed into service. The Union, which joined the Labour Party, the General Federation of Trade Unions and the Cooperative Union in a 'War Emergency Workers' National Committee' fought against dilution of the profession and tried to head off panicky local authorities which felt a patriotic call to make educational economies.

By 1916, the year of the Somme, it was quite obvious that the union's laudable self restraint over salaries no longer fitted the facts and there was growing impatience among local associations. War bonuses and the shortage of labour were improving earnings generally; one of the educational effects was a noteworthy increase in the number of children whose parents could afford to let them stay beyond the normal leaving age. At the same time the Board, anxious about staffing trends, was converted to the view that there had to be a substantial improvement in salaries. In October 1916 the Union executive resolved to 'initiate and develop a national movement to secure an immediate and substantial increase in salaries'. In May 1917 H. A. L. Fisher, the President of the Board, said that he contemplated using the Board's new powers to prescribe a minimum salary of £100 for certificated men teachers, £90 for certificated women, and £65 for uncertificated women. From then on, with the Board committed to intervention, there was a wave of strikes among teachers from 1917 to 1919; the stage was set for the establishment of the Burnham negotiating machinery.

The First World War, like the Boer War and the Second World War, provided the common idealism and a national interest for the general improvement of the education system. The fact that teachers themselves benefited from this – Fisher put through a valuable Superannuation Act in 1918 – was almost incidental as far as the public was concerned. Lloyd George, looking forward to a 'land fit for heroes', applauded the idea of a new Education Act. H. A. L. Fisher, who brought forward the 1918 measure which ensured a school leaving age of 14 (thus abolishing the half time system) and reformed the grants system, was cheered by a mass meeting of Bristol dockers in the course of a speaking tour to raise enthusiasm for his Bill. Unhappily, compared with either 1902 or 1944, the Fisher Act was to do little for Britain's children.

By 1918 the union had a membership of over 100,000; a significant decision by the 1919 conference to let in uncertificated teachers – in reality the triumph of certificated teachers in their own profession – added a further 11,000. After half a century there was still much that was wrong with British education: elementary schools left a lot to be desired, the organisation of secondary schools was unsatisfactory, and the chances of an ex-elementary student reaching university were tiny. But the NUT had done much to raise standards, it had some brilliant leaders and its political machine was the fear or envy of others. It stood ready to fight for education in both the darker and the brighter years ahead.

# Bradford pioneers school welfare

A special interest in health and fitness sprang partly from the Boer War, when thousands of young men were rejected as being unfit for service. A committee on Physical Deterioration was set up which reported in 1904 that it was 'the height of cruelty to subject half-starved children to the processes of education.' In 1906 an Act empowered authorities to spend money out of the rates to feed necessitous children. The first to do so was Bradford, who took over the pioneering organisation begun by Margaret McMillan. This outstanding woman had served as an Independent Labour member of the Bradford School Board. The pictures in the next four pages, taken in 1907, shows that from the first, the Bradford School Meals Service was a very well organised concern.

Bradford, too, was the first to establish a general school clinic for medical treatment. In 1907 a medical department was set up at the Board of Education with Sir George Newman at its head. Its annual reports did a great deal to bring about better medical facilities for school-children. From 1907 all children were inspected on entering and leaving school. The Union urged that medical treatment should be made compulsory after inspection, but this was not achieved until 1918.

1. Margaret McMillan, who declared that education was failing because 'the bottom rungs are rotten'. With her sister Rachel, she pioneered nursery education in London after leaving Bradford.

2. These were some of the poverty-stricken children who roused her compassion. They were photographed at the Bradford Parish Church School in 1900.

1. White Abbey Wesleyan School, which was closed when Green Lane School was opened in 1903, was used as one of the first dining centres in 1907. The children from Green Lane School and others in the district attended there. In charge and shown here was Jonathan Priestley, the first headmaster of Green Lane School and the father of J. B. Priestley. Dr Dessian, teacher of German at Belle Vue School, is wearing the white apron. The Union had secured in the Feeding of Children Act that teachers would not be compelled to supervise school meals, but the response from Bradford teachers to help voluntarily was overwhelming. The education committee later offered them an acknowledgment of sixpence per day.

2. Mr. Priestley weighs the children, helped by Miss Marion Cuff, the organiser of domestic subjects.

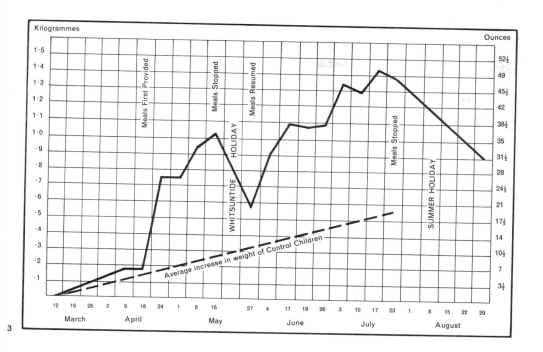

**3**

Kilogrammes / Ounces

Meals First Provided
Meals Stopped
Meals Resumed
HOLIDAY
WHITSUNTIDE
Meals Stopped
SUMMER HOLIDAY

Average increase in weight of Control Children

12 19 26 | 2 9 16 24 | 1 8 16 | 27 4 11 19 26 | 3 10 17 23 | 1 8 15 22 29
March | April | May | June | July | August

**4**

**5**

3. The results were dramatic. This graph, submitted to the Education Committee, showed the increase in weight in children receiving school meals, compared with the 'control group'. The gain was immediately lost during school holidays when the children returned to a semi-starvation diet. The Bradford Authority accordingly began to provide meals during the holidays. The expenditure was disallowed year after year by the government auditor and Bradford paid for it out of the profits of the gas undertaking.

4. and 5. Equipment and staff in the central kitchen. The cost of food for one child's meal was 1·31d.

1. This ingenious system of tubs was devised to allow individual bathing. Most centres in Bradford were equipped with double (shower) baths.

2. Motor lorries were used to deliver meals to other schools. Mr. Priestley complained regularly in the logbook about having lorries in the schoolyard.

3. In London, poor children waiting for free dinners. By 1910, only 100 authorities were providing school meals out of the rates, and private charity still had to supplement them.

# Towards a healthier generation

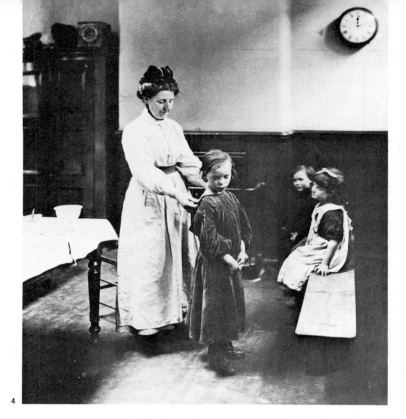

4. A London school-girl receiving a medical inspection in 1912.

5. Special education for handicapped children was beginning. This was the Oral Deaf and Dumb Institute in London.

# The scars of war

It is a striking fact that three major Education Acts have been passed in wartime – 1902, 1918, and 1944. A major struggle shows up social deficiencies and hastens existing trends. In 1914, educational reform was in the air, but the 1918 Act contained more far-reaching proposals than were planned in 1914.

War disrupted the educational system cruelly. Schools were requisitioned, children were taken from school to work, and, above all, half the male teachers joined the armed forces. Yet schools remained open, though many resorted to a 'double shift' system of part-time education for twice the number of children. The school meals service expanded considerably to enable mothers to work.

At the outbreak of the War, the Union suspended its salaries campaign in the national interest. But wartime conditions brought full employment, higher wages and a rising cost of living, accentuating the low salaries paid to teachers. In 1916, the salary campaign was renewed and the Union secured the 'Fisher grant' which enabled LEAs to pay a war bonus to serving teachers.

1

2

3

4

1 and 2. Teachers were to the fore in answering the call to arms; indeed the Board of Education initially tried to dissuade too many from joining up. In 1915, the Union inaugurated a War Aid Fund for the benefit of teachers serving in the forces and their dependants. Several V.C.s were awarded to teachers.

3. School children shared in the popular excitement at the beginning of the war. War had not yet impinged on civilian life, and there was little realisation of the long and bloody struggle ahead.

4. The harsh reality. Schoolgirls at the graves of air-raid victims in Folkestone.

1. 'School gardens' were one contribution to the war effort. Teachers also organised thrift campaigns.

2. Shortages of food, fuel and clothing affected children severely. *The Schoolmaster* published weekly lessons on how to use coal economically.

3. The overcrowded schools had to expand a little further to accommodate young Belgian refugees.

# High hopes dashed by the money squeeze

It was 1919, and according to the NUT it was *annus mirabilis*. A year earlier, the 1918 Education Act sponsored by H. A. L. Fisher, president of the Board of Education, had passed through Parliament; and W. P. Folland, president of the NUT, was so moved by what he described as the Act's realisation of the Child's Charter of Freedom, which had been so warmly espoused by the Union, that he ended his address to Conference by quoting Jerusalem.

Over the next 25 years, the vision of Blake was often used by leaders of the NUT. As usual, Jerusalem always seemed to hover tantalisingly on the educational horizon. Occasionally, as in 1919, it seemed to have arrived. Yet within months it had been redefined, the Treasury had started to cut back spending, and it seemed yet again a distant objective that educationists should work towards. Such was the mood in the early years after the passing of the Fisher Act.

So many of its causes had been enshrined in the 1918 Act, however, that the NUT had every reason for its early euphoria. The act improved the administrative organisation of education, secured for every child an un-impeded life in elementary school until 14, established part-time day continuation schools (which never got started except in Rugby), made a series of proposals for developing the senior end of education, consolidated elementary school grants and surveyed the total educational provision of the country. Above all, it laid the foundations of a national education system.

It also added to the Government's powers to stimulate local education authorities, reformed the grant system, abolished the half-time system and fees in elementary schools, and empowered education authorities to raise the school-leaving age to 15 (which took another 30 years in most areas). It permitted authorities to open nursery schools, and it laid down that elementary school classes should consist of a maximum of 60 pupils (though such a size should not be tolerated), and that secondary classes should never exceed 35. The Act also introduced and enshrined the philosophy of equality of opportunity, which was to become the major issue of the next 30 years, when it said: 'Children shall not be debarred from receiving the benefits of any form of education by which they are capable of profiting through inability to pay fees'.

The crucial clause was stated in Section One: 'With a view to the establishment of a national system of public education for all persons capable of profiting thereby, it shall be the *duty* of the council of every county and county borough, so far as their powers extend, to contribute thereto by providing for the progressive development

and comprehensive organisation of education in respect of their area, and with that object any such council may and shall, when required by the Board of Education, submit schemes showing the mode in which their duties and powers under the Education Acts shall be performed and exercised'.

The ideology, and the theme that was to recur constantly until it was more prominently stated in 1944, was put eloquently by Mr Fisher when he spoke in the Commons in August 1917, and discussed the 'social solidarity' created by the war. After a war in which the poor had been asked to pour out their blood, he said, every just mind began to realise that the boundaries of citizenship were not determined by wealth, and that the logic that led to an extension of the franchise led also to an extension of education.

He went on:

*'There is a growing sense . . . that the industrial workers of the country are entitled to be considered primarily as citizens and as fit subjects for any form of education from which they are capable of profiting. I notice also that a new way of thinking about education has sprung up among the more reflecting members of our industrial army. They do not want education only in order that they may become better technical workmen and earn higher wages. They do not want it in order that they may rise out of their own class, always a vulgar ambition. They want it because they know that in the treasures of the mind they can find an aid to good citizenship, a source of pure enjoyment, and a refuge from the necessary hardships of a life spent in the midst of clanging machinery in our hideous cities of toil'.*

Yet by 1920, the NUT was already re-defining its concept of Jerusalem. Whatever the promises of the 1918 act, there were still heights to scale and peaks to gain, Miss Jane Wood told the annual conference in Margate in her presidential address. At that stage, 24 years before the next Act, she outlined the philosophy that was afterwards advocated constantly by the NUT and which was eventually to be the spirit of the Butler Act. Perhaps the greatest and most pressing task, she said, was to secure equality of opportunity in the education system for all.

The detailed statistics in the report buttressed the arguments that had been advanced by the NUT. It pointed out, for instance, that about a half of the 14 to 15 year olds and three out of five of the 15 to 16 year olds in the country were not getting any full-time education at all. Out of 3,600,000 children of 11 to 16, more than half in 1922–23 were in elementary schools. Only 265,000 (7·2 per cent) were in grant-aided secondary schools and 12,000 in junior technical schools. At the age of 13 to 14, only 88 per cent of children were attending school.

Arguing the case for raising the school leaving age, the report said that there was a proved social and intellectual deterioration resulting from the premature entry of many thousands of young persons into wage-earning employment, as well as the waste of part of the effort and money applied to the early stages of children's lives. 'It may be urged', the report said, 'that it is unreasonable to incur the burden of prolonging education at a period of great economic depression. It may be equally urged that it is unreasonable to attempt to harvest crops in spring, or to divert into supplying the economic necessities of the immediate present the still undeveloped capacities of those on whose intelligence and character the very life of the nation must depend in the future. There is no capital more productive than the energies of human beings. There is no investment more re-munerative than expenditure devoted to developing them'.

Two years later, the Board of Education issued *The New Prospect in Education*, which showed that the arguments in the Hadow Report had been persuasive. 'It is important', the Board said, 'to grasp the fact that the Report has in mind *all* sorts and conditions of children, the humble and the weak as well as the mighty and the strong, and that to concentrate especially on a erection of a few splendidly-equipped schools for selected children is to miss the real lesson'.

'The advance contemplated is not on a narrow and selective front, but the whole line is to move forward'.

The NUT, which also published a detailed reaction to the report, agreed almost wholly with the recommendations. A 71-page docu-ment ended with 55 NUT proposals, among them a suggestion for experiments with multiple bias schools, the early forerunners of the comprehensive school, and a warning about the dangers involved in selection at 11 plus. It added that sufficient time and attention should be devoted to arts and crafts and music, as well as to language teaching; that no class should exceed 40; supported the raising of the school-leaving age and urged the abolition of fees for secondary education; and said that if any distinction was to be made at 11 plus, it was the humble and the weak who should get special attention, for they were the least able to help themselves. 'The teachers of the country accept with a few reservations the changes that are now proposed' the Union said, 'not because the new system is likely to be perfect, but because it provides a base from which a further and outstanding advance may be made'.

The second Hadow Report, published in 1931, shaped primary education for the next 20 years; indicated the psychological thinking that changed the old elementary school into the modern primary school; endorsed a break at seven plus for entry to junior school, and at 11 plus for entry to secondary school; and discussed research supporting the concept of streaming pupils by the age of ten. The central statement of its section on the curriculum, still of interest today in the light of some of the allegations about 'modern'

Several classes at work in one classroom. Economic difficulties severely affected school building in the inter-war period.

methods, was: 'We are of the opinion that the curriculum of the primary school is to be thought of in terms of activity and experience rather than of knowledge to be acquired and facts to be stored'. It also demanded a maximum size of class of 40, parental co-operation, improved school building standards, and the training of teachers for backward groups.

[Seven years later, under Sir Will Spens, the Consultative Committee again endorsed the 'ages and stages' pattern of the two Hadow Reports, and recommended an expansion of technical schools; the continued expansion of secondary education in grammar, modern and technical schools (as well as experiments with all three on the same site); parity of staffing between secondary schools; the raising of the school-leaving age to 16; and the introduction of courses based on senior pupils' vocational interests. As was to happen in the 1960s, the agenda for the next leap forward had been outlined.]

Meanwhile, although its eyes were constantly on the horizon, the Union was continually called on to defend the interests of its members and of the nation's schools. The slump was imminent and two reports from the Committee on National Expenditure – the May and Ray reports – recommended severe cuts in the education budget. One showed just how necessary was the determined stand taken by the NUT, as well, perhaps, as the progress that was being made.

'Since the standard of education, elementary and secondary, that is being given to the children of poor parents', it said, 'is already in very many cases superior to that which the middle-class parent is providing for his own child, we feel that it is time to pause'.

As the slump progressed, schools were closed, school building was suspended, and in October 1932, when more than 7,000 unqualified teachers were in service, 1,100 newly-qualified teachers were unemployed. The NUT fought to protect their interests. Yet it was also still looking ahead, and it launched a campaign under the banner 'Free secondary education for all capable of profiting by it'. Once the slump was passed, moreover, spending on education picked up and there was a flurry of activity from the Board. A bill was introduced for the raising of the school leaving age by 1939, though parents were able to opt out. Spending of £12m on technical education was sanctioned. It issued circulars on school building, nursery schools, school transport, medical services and physical training.

After the death of King George V in 1935, and only a few years before the outbreak of war, which was to offer once again the impetus for a major reform, the Board of Education issued a survey of the progress of education since 1910. It showed on the one hand that there had certainly been progress. Yet on the other it showed that the NUT was justified in saying clamourously that still more was needed. Among the points that it made were:—

The cooperative partnership between central and local government, adumbrated in the 1918 act, had become an established fact, and there was less detailed control from Whitehall.

One and three-quarter million new school places had been built.

There were 38,000 classes of more than 50 in 1920, including 7,000 with more than 60. Now there were only 4,262, of which only 44 were of more than 60.

A comprehensive plan for the advanced education of the mass of the nation's children had been carried already halfway to completion. In 1935, nearly 800,000 pupils (41 per cent) older than 11 were in senior departments compared with 163,000 (8·5 per cent) in 1927.

The average salary of a man teacher had increased from £199 to £404, and of a woman from £133 to £311 in the same period; and the percentage of graduates from 54 to 78 per cent.

The number of school medical officers had increased from 995 to 1,412, of school dentists from 27 to 852, of school nurses from 436 to 3,429 and of medical inspections from one to three million.

Six causes of progress were identified by the Board:—
The new fact of public control, which it said was the most fundamental.
Proper financial provision for school building and maintenance.
Effective internal organisation following the regulation of age and conditions of entry.
The development of a reasonable system of examinations, which afforded a test of ordinary school work to which the whole of appropriate forms were submitted and not just selected pupils.
The development of sixth form work and its effect on the whole school.
Above all and the most essential, the growth of a body of teachers, better educated, more generally interested in their work, and – though much remained to be done in this respect – with fuller opportunities for learning the technique of their profession.

At the outbreak of war, the Union was thrown into a maelstrom of activity. Union headquarters were removed to Toddington Manor in Gloucestershire and Union staff performed heroic labours on behalf of the schools, children and teachers who were evacuated to the country. Yet in spite of its pre-occupation with the war, the NUT had already started its campaign for the new Education Act when the first Conference of the war was held in 1942. Over the next three years, and under the vigorous leadership of Sir Fred Mander, general secretary, and Mr Ronald Gould, president of the Union in 1943 and eventual successor to Mander, the Union was seen at its most effective and, perhaps, at the most significant period of its whole history: an insistent, powerful and influential force for educational progress. Its stamp was recognisably set on the resultant act, which was, in fact, largely the work of Sir Fred Mander, Sir Percival Sharpe, secretary of the Association of Education Committees, and Sir Maurice Holmes, Permanent Secretary to the Board of Education. The contribution of the Union was recognised by Mr Churchill when he said that because of the activities of the NUT: 'The people have been rendered conscious that they are coming into their inheritance'.

The NUT campaign had been initiated at a meeting at Central Hall, Westminster, in 1941, the year when the Board's draft proposals for the Act were circulated in a draft form. Soon, the Union joined forces with the Workers' Educational Association and the TUC in the Council for Educational

Advance, and in 1942, it published the 'sage green book', its 45-page document, Educational Reconstruction. The document had been approved by the Conference and was the summation of the policies that the Union had advocated since the 1920s.

'The Executive of the NUT' 'are profoundly convinced that equal educational opportunity for all must be an essential characteristic of any state system of education for this country if it is to continue its democratic form of government'. They wish, however, to state clearly what they understand by equality of opportunity. It is the application of the principle 'that the accidents of parental circumstances or of the place of residence shall not preclude any child from receiving the education from which he is best capable of profiting'.

No-one would seriously suggest that there is equality of opportunity in this country today. The need for change is therefore patent ... There is one change which must be effected before the system can afford any degree of equality between children in schools even in the same town or district. Consequent upon the method of development of the state system of education, there has grown up within it a caste system, which should find no place in any national scheme of education.

'This is exemplified in a number of ways. The type of school determines the standards of accommodation, the character of the amenities provided, the normal length of school life, the salaries of teachers engaged and even the fees which have to be paid. By common consent, the statutory and administrative distinction between elementary and higher education, which corresponds to no educational distinction, is a deplorable weakness of the present system. But it is not the only one. The fact that a child's educational prospects are largely determined by the geographical location of his home is another, and this calls loudly for remedy'.

The two aims, the NUT said, should be the creation of the conditions needed to afford

The last meeting of the executive of the NUT attended by Sir James Yoxall before his retirement in 1922.

equality of opportunity and a greater unification of the educational system. Its detailed recommendations included the establishment of nursery education from two, a school life until 16, the abolition of fees for secondary education, a single code of regulations for all secondary schools, provision for further education until 18, annual medical inspections, a duty on education authorities to provide free school meals, a trained and graduate teaching profession, a single authority for all primary and secondary education, and a unified, local administration system for the education service. Almost all of the recommendations were included in the Act.

A year later, the Board, under the joint leadership of R. A. Butler and Chuter Ede, published its White Paper on Educational Reconstruction. The Government's purpose, it said, was to secure for children a happier childhood and a better start in life; to secure a fuller measure of education and opportunity for young people, and to provide means for all to develop the various talents with which they were endowed, and so enriching the inheritance of the country whose citizens they were.

'The new educational opportunities must not, therefore, be of a single pattern. It is just as important to achieve diversity as it is to ensure equality of educational opportunity. But such diversity must not impair the social unity within the education system which will open the way to a more closely knit society and give us strength to face the tasks ahead. In the youth of the nation we have our greatest national asset. Even on a basis of mere expediency, we cannot afford not to develop this asset to the greatest advantage'.

It went on to set out the following agenda for the Act:—
A sufficient supply of nursery schools.
The raising of the school-leaving age to 15, and then to 16 as soon as circumstances allowed.
Primary education until 11.
Secondary education, of diversified types but of equal standing, for all children.
At primary level, the large classes and bad conditions which were a reproach to the system would be systematically eliminated.

At secondary level, the standard of accommodation and amenities would be raised in all schools to the level of the best examples.
School meals and milk would be made obligatory.
There would be medical inspection and treatment without charge.
Provision for part-time education until 18.

The NUT nevertheless continued its campaign. The annual conference approved the step in the White Paper towards equality of opportunity in the system, but regretted that a firm date for the raising of the school leaving age to 16 had been omitted, that all secondary education was not made free of fees, and that statutory provision had not been made for reducing the size of classes.

Offering the NUT in 1943 an early indication of his oratorical ability, Ronald Gould, the president, described what was still wrong with the education system.

'It provides unequal opportunities in schools of unequal social standing', he declared, 'giving courses of unequal length under unequal conditions. Such a state of affairs is socially evil and morally reprehensible. If equality of opportunity is anything more than a catchword, it must be made to mean exactly what it says. We must provide equal opportunities, in schools of equal social standing, giving courses of equal duration under equivalent conditions. This means the ending of shabby treatment for the many and the sharing of privileges by all'.

A special national assembly was called in London in November to start an intensive, sustained and nationwide campagn for the introduction of the Bill, at which both Gould and Mander delivered inspiring addresses to the troops. Mander explained that the Union had moved now into a political situation and ended, in a good example of the sort of oratory that spiced the conferences of the inter-war years: 'I would that I had the silver tongue of a McNamara and could fire you as he did in days of old'. Then I would say to you: 'Be strong for the child, gird up your loins, quit you like men'. Meetings were held throughout the country, both by the NUT and the CEA, and a Watching Committee was established to supervise the passage of the bill through parliament.

The Act which eventually received the Royal Assent embodied the proposals of the 1943 White Paper, as well as the reforms that had been advocated by the NUT. It was greeted by G. C. T. Giles, president of the Union in 1944, as a great step forward towards a democratic system of education, embodying a new and worthier conception of the value and purpose of education.

Aiming for the summit of Snowdon are delegates at the 1939 conference held at Llandudno.

The Act replaced and reformed almost all law relating to education since 1870 and offered Free Secondary Education for All as its main promise. Its main provisions were:—

A new authority over education was assigned to the state and the newly-titled Minister of Education was empowered to secure the effective execution by local authorities, under his control and direction, of the national policy for education.

The old arrangement of elementary and higher education was replaced by 'a continuous process conducted in three stages' of primary, secondary and further education.

The county and county borough councils were made responsible for all stages and local education authorities were given the duty to secure adequate provision of primary and secondary education, including nursery and special schools, and to prepare development plans. Tuition fees in state schools were forbidden.

The dual system, the side-by-side existence of schools provided by education authorities and the Churches, was modified, but the voluntary bodies were offered generous financial help.

The day in all state schools was to begin with a corporate act of worship and religious instruction in state schools was to be given according to the syllabus agreed by the religious denominations.

The school-leaving age was raised to 15.

The former legal duty of parents to cause their children to get efficient elementary instruction in the three Rs was replaced by a duty to ensure that their children got efficient full-time education suited to their age, aptitudes and abilities.

Statutory backing was given to the Burnham Committee and the Minister was empowered to make its scales mandatory on education authorities. It also enacted equal pay for women.

Education authorities were given welfare functions, including medical inspection, free medical and dental treatment, milk, meals and other refreshment, and the provision of free clothing and scholarships for higher education.

Authorities were given the duty of providing compulsory part-time education equivalent to one day a week in County Colleges for those under 18 who were not in full-time education.

The act was a triumphant vindication of the NUT's efforts since 1918 and its passing amounted, perhaps, to its finest hour.

**The religious controversy**

Although it dominated the debate immediately before the 1944 Act, the controversy over religious education and instruction needs a book in itself. Yet the role of the NUT, and especially of Sir Fred Mander, was crucial in the compromise that was eventually adopted by Mr Butler.

Mander had succeeded to the General Secretaryship of the Union in 1929 after he had impressed the annual conference with a passionate declaration that there should be no yielding to the Churches by teachers during a religious controversy which was going on at the time. Yet later he became much more concerned about educational development than the religious issue, and at the time when the new Act was under preparation he was so concerned to achieve the educational advance that he considered essential, and in particular, Secondary Education for All, that he was content to accept almost any compromise solution that would enable the Act to get on to the Statute Book with the educational reforms that the NUT wanted.

The controversy erupted in 1941 when the Archbishops of Canterbury, York and Wales issued a public statement emphasising their concern that schools should instruct pupils in a Christian view of life. At this stage, Mander wrote a crucial series of five articles in *The Schoolmaster* setting out the grounds for a solution of the argument.

Teachers, he declared, saw no reason whatsoever why the Archbishops should continue to call the tune in schools maintained though not provided by the local authorities and to call the tune, with the help of Free Churchmen, in schools both maintained and provided out of public money. They felt even more strongly when certain of the suggestions might threaten their professional interests on such vital points as appointment, dismissal, tenure, promotion, and even freedom of conscience. So long as it was teachers and not the Churches who were called on to give the instruction, it was teachers and not the churches who were pivotal to the whole position. 'The idea of religious instruction given in state schools

under duress in accordance with a scheme imposed from outside in opposition to the reasonable rights and wishes of teachers is unthinkable', he wrote. 'It would mark the beginning of the end to religious instruction in the schools'.

The major points of the solution he proposed were:—

A national syllabus recommended by the Board for adoption as a basic of the scheme of instruction in schools.

A freeing of the timetable so that teachers who did not want to teach r.i. were freed from it.

Abolition of the right of entry by the Churches and inspection by HMIs.

Voluntary schools should be transferred ideally to local authorities but with due safeguards for trust deed teaching.

Safeguards on any test of the religious credentials of teachers.

A disclaimer by the Churches of any desire to inspect.

Such in the end was largely the basis of the NUT's submission to the Government, and, as the clauses in the Act show, several were accepted. Yet the triumph belonged to Mr Butler. He proposed a solution which nobody thought satisfactory, but which gave all parties something they wanted, and which none of them could reject. Ever since the controversy has died down.

# The Act that partly failed

1. Mr H. A. L. Fisher arriving for the opening of Parliament in 1919. An eminent historian and Vice-Chancellor of the University of Sheffield, he was appointed President of the Board of Education by Lloyd George in 1917. He quickly utilised the prevailing climate of social reform to introduce his far-reaching measures. 'The war was my opportunity', he later said.

The 1918 Act and its partner, the Teachers' Superannuation Act, were hailed by the Union as a crowning of its efforts. But the economic blizzard that hit the nation three years later made it a partial failure. The Act established a universal leaving-age of 14, abolished the half-time system, strengthened local authorities, and extended the meals and medical services. It also planned a school-leaving age of 15, day continuation classes for all up to 18, and the provision of nursery schools; these clauses proved inoperable.

1

2

2. The building was specially built for Rugby's continuation school. The idea of continuation classes had been borrowed from Germany. Children who left school at 14 were to attend classes for a minimum of 320 hours every year – day release, in effect. It was to be compulsory up to 16 at first and up to 18 after seven years. In the event, not even the first part got off the ground. Only the school in Rugby survived.

A major factor in its success was the number of new electrical industries in Rugby who appreciated well-educated labour. After a useful life it finally closed in 1969.

3. The Union continued to press for nursery schools for the under-fives to be established, as allowed by the Act, but very few were.

3

# The beginning of Burnham

Soon after the passage of the Education Act and Superannuation Act, Fisher tackled the problem of teachers' salaries, which had been so dramatically highlighted during the war. He dismissed the first idea of civil service status as endangering educational freedom and instead arrived at the solution of the Burnham Committees. The Elementary Schools Committee recommended a scale that meant that, because of the steep rise in the cost of living, the teachers were actually slightly worse off in real terms than they had been in 1914. But at least the worst anomalies were removed as the LEAs were forced by the NUT to accept the scale. The NUT wisely refused a scale based on the cost of living and thus gained as prices fell from 1921 onwards.

1. Viscount Burnham, who chaired the joint committees and gave his name to them.

2. The Elementary Schools Committee was made up of representatives of the NUT and the LEA associations. This was the standard scale they suggested in 1920. Many graduates, including those who had taken four-year courses in day training colleges, taught in public elementary schools.

### Scale for Certificated Teachers.

3. (a) Certificated Assistant Teachers, Two Years College Trained :—

| Scale. | Men. | | | Women. | | |
|---|---|---|---|---|---|---|
| | Minimum. | Annual Increment. | Maximum. | Minimum. | Annual Increment. | Maximum. |
| Standard Scale I. - - - | £ $172\frac{1}{2}$ | £ $12\frac{1}{2}$ | £ 325 | £ 160 | £ $12\frac{1}{2}$ | £ 260 |

(b) There shall be added to the Minimum—

(i) one increment for Certificated Teachers who either have completed a three years' continuous period of training or are graduates of a British University;

(ii) two increments for Certificated Teachers who are graduates of British Universities, and have also completed a four years' continuous period of training.

(c) For other Certificated Assistant Teachers, except as provided in Section 14 of the Standard Scales Report, the Minimum shall be less than that stated in (a) above by the amount of one increment in each case, the maximum remaining unaltered.

(d) Married Teachers—

In cases in which a husband and wife, both being Certificated Teachers, have been appointed or are appointed to posts in the same school or department, and where the requirements of the Board of Education as to staffing can be met by the appointment of an Assistant Teacher who is not Certificated, the salary of the husband (if he be the Assistant Teacher) or of the wife (if she be the Assistant Teacher) shall be that attaching to the status of the Assistant Teacher required.

# The Geddes axe falls

'The educational year which dawned full of hope is closing amidst doubt, uncertainty and gloom.' The 1921 presidential address by G. H. Powell was the first of many gloomy comments by Union Leaders. In the economic depression of the inter-war years, the NUT battled to protect education and their own position against government cuts. Their comparative success in preserving salaries in a period of falling prices and their freedom from mass unemployment meant that the profession achieved a higher status by the end of the thirties.

"A CLOSE CUT"

3

3. Teachers had to accept several 'voluntary' cuts in their salary, each one of which was stoutly opposed by the Union. This wry comment was drawn by a Kent teacher in 1926. Lord Eustace Percy was President of the Board of Education and Winston Churchill was Chancellor of the Exchequer in the Conservative government of 1924 to 1929. Percy is saying to Winnie 'She looks jolly nice with that cut'.

4. Unemployed dockers – a picture that mirrors the greyness of the depressed areas. Newly qualified teachers, particularly in Wales, found great difficulty in finding their first post. The Union paid them until they had succeeded.

4

1. In 1931 a 10 per cent cut was imposed – it would have been 15 per cent if the Union had not intervened. In 1933 the NUT and the Educational Institute of Scotland organised a mammoth petition to demand a restitution of the lost salary. More than 210,000 signatures were received and they were delivered to Number 10 Downing Street (occupied by Ramsay MacDonald). The cut was not restored until 1935.

2. The members of the joint delegation of the NUT and the EIS which presented the petition. In the back row (left to right) are Miss A. B. Muir, Mr H. Humphreys, Mr Hugh B. Guthrie, and Miss M. Gardner, all of the NUT. In the front are Mr Thomas Henderson, General Secretary of the EIS, Mr Charles W. Thomson, President of the EIS, Mr H. N. Penlington, President of the NUT and Mr F. Mander (later Sir Frederick Mander), General Secretary of the NUT.

1

3

3. One of the main casualties of the government squeeze was the raising of the school leaving age to 15. The NUT constantly urged that it should be implemented, and one argument they used was that it would help to solve the serious problem of unemployed youngsters. In 1936, a definite commitment was made which would have come into effect on September 1, 1939, but on that day Germany invaded Poland, and it was again postponed. This junior instruction centre in Sunderland was one of many established by local authorities to give some sort of craft instruction to school-leavers until they found a job.

# Secondary education for all – but how?

All children now stayed on at school until 14, but for most their entire school life was spent in one elementary school. Then, too, the secondary grammar schools could no longer accommodate all pupils qualified to enter. The Hadow Report in 1926 suggested three main solutions, besides reiterating the need for a school-leaving age of 15. It advocated the reorganisation of all-age elementary schools into separate junior and senior schools; it gave official sanction, now backed by psychological evidence, to the transfer age of 11 which had evolved after 1902; and it proposed that another type of post-primary education should be developed alongside the grammar schools, based on the existing technical and central schools.

By the time the Spens Committee reported in 1939, a system of grammar, modern and technical schools had emerged, and with it came a philosophy of aptitudes which held that children could be assigned to different schools at 11 according to their bent for academic study, applied science or art, or practical work. Though welcoming the extension of post-primary education to all pupils, the NUT increasingly questioned the wisdom of segregation into different types of schools, which would never, despite official protestations, be regarded as equal. From Hadow onwards they urged that experiments in multi-bias schools, the fore-runners of comprehensives, should be encouraged. The Spens Report studied this proposition very seriously but reluctantly turned it down on considerations of excessive size and difficulty in maintaining academic standards – arguments that were later to become very familiar in the comprehensive debate.

4. A chemical laboratory in a grammar school. The main criticism of grammar school education in this period was of the excessive influence of the School Certificate Examination, and the Norwood Committee in 1943 suggested a new examination structure. The NUT sought to have fees entirely abolished but, once again, the nation's economic plight made this impossible.

5. Nature study in a central school. Central schools, as we have seen, had grown up before 1914 in a rather devious way to meet the demand for secondary education and had only received official recognition in the 1918 Act. Their bias was practical but not purely vocational, and they fitted well into the philosophy for 'modern' schools laid down by Hadow. Their pupils were selected at 11 at a lower standard than for grammar schools. A curious anomaly was that they were still governed by the Elementary Code and not the Secondary Code. The NUT tried hard to have one code adopted for all schools but without success until 1944.

4    5

1. A woodwork class in a junior technical school. Again, junior technical schools had been established before the war, mainly in industrial centres in the North. They took pupils at 13 for a curriculum based on the techniques of local industries, but, as distinct from 'trade schools', they did not set out to train for specific jobs. The standard reached was usually higher than in central schools. The Spens Report was very enthusiastic about their work, and recommended that they should take pupils at 11.

2. Boys learning the craft of bookbinding in a senior school. Senior schools had developed before 1914, as non-selective central schools. They catered for pupils who had failed to gain a place in the other three types of schools, and their function was to a large extent remedial. Craftwork played a very important part in the curriculum. Teachers had to take this in their stride without any specialised training, and the standard reached was a tribute to their enthusiasm.

## From elementary to junior

Elementary schools were now known as junior
schools. The change from all-age schools gave
a greater coherence and freedom to teaching,
and the modern primary school began to
emerge. But the eleven plus selection became
increasingly important and in some ways it
meant an unwelcome return to external
examinations which had been one of the
bugbears of 'payment by results'. Streaming
was accepted by the 1931 Hadow Report on
primary education as a necessary feature of the
junior school.

3

3. Hadow reorganisation was difficult to achieve
in rural areas because of the large areas
involved. In many cases senior classes or
'higher tops' had to remain within the same
building as the junior school. But where
centralised schools were set up, school buses
made their appearance. The Rutland
Committee adopted a different solution. They
gave grants to parents to buy bicycles for their
children.

4. Cyril Burt, professor of psychology at
University College, London, from 1931 to 1950,
supported the importance of 'the general factor
of intelligence' as against 'aptitudes'. Tests
devised by Burt had been used as early as 1919
in Bradford as part of the 'eleven plus', with the
aim of overcoming environmental factors.
Many authorities adopted standardised tests in
English, Arithmetic and Intelligence, but
selection procedures were still anything but
uniform.

5. A vivid portrait of an all-age school. In 1922,
all the pupils at the Llantwit Fardre Council
School in Glamorgan were photographed in
the playground. The occasion was the retiral of
their headmaster Mr William Chubb, the
dignified gentleman in the bowler hat.

4

5

# More child-centred teaching

Educational theory was in the air. The apostles of 'child-centred education' – Dewey, Froebel and Montessori – were having an increasing impact on teaching.

'Activity' learning was most apparent in the infant departments particularly in the Montessori classes set up in many schools, but in every type of school, teaching methods were more fluid, and practical work more important. Extra-curricular activities such as school orchestras and clubs flourished. The 1918 Act had allowed LEAs to spend money on school camps, swimming baths, and playing fields, and many took advantage of this dispensation.

1

2

1. A Montessori class in an infant school. The 1931 Report on primary education recognized seven plus as the best age of transfer from infant school or department to junior school.

2. A shop to practise arithmetic in an infant school.

3. A needlework class. Teachers often had to improvise with imperfect equipment and accommodation to widen the curriculum.

4. Boys at a senior school working out the height of their school as a practical application of classroom mathematics.

4

5. 'Housewifery centres' were included in many
new schools.

6 and 7. The gramophone and the wireless
made their contribution to teaching methods.

8. Learning how the engine of a motor-car
works.

# A place in the sun

In a reaction to the overcrowded slums of the old towns, the nation developed a passion for fresh air. The new schools to match the new housing estates were much more open. Classes were frequently held outside, and children were sent, for short and long periods, to open-air schools.

1

1. Schools typically, were built round an open quadrangle, where earlier it would have been the school hall. School-building was of course badly hit by the recurring squeezes and a Black List of below-standard schools originally drawn up by the Board of Education in 1908 and revised in 1927 was only slowly reduced. Classrooms often had one side that could be opened out completely.

2. An open-air school in St James's Park in 1927. At the height of the enthusiasm for open-air learning, there were 170 classes being regularly held in London parks all the year round, using bandstands as their only refuge in wet weather. Most were for normal children, but one well-known one, in Regent's Park, was started in 1911 for tubercular children. They were given clogs to keep their feet dry, rugs to cover them, and in the depths of winter, slow combustion foot-warmers.

2

3

4

3. An open-air school for tubercular children. Before the development of modern drugs, fresh air, sunshine, and rest were the only palliatives for the disease. In 1930, the LCC alone had seven open-air day schools. With the open wooden buildings substantially rebuilt, they now serve as schools for delicate children.

4. After the 1918 Act, the provision of school meals increased, but still only a very small percentage of children benefited. The emphasis was still far more on need than on meals as part of a general education. This picture shows how many rural schools, where the demand was greater because of the long distances now to be travelled, had to cope without a dining-room. These children paid 1s 3d per week for their meals, which were cooked in the cookery room and served by the children.

5. Some authorities began to issue free milk, mainly to the youngest classes.

5

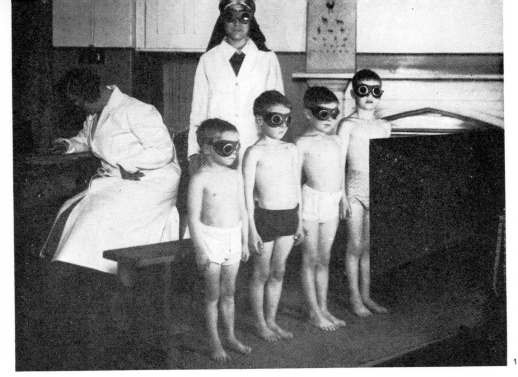

1. Medical treatment was now compulsory following inspection. Ultra-violet ray treatment was in fashion.

2. Boys learning to cook in a special school for backward children. Special education was still largely concerned with the needs of physically handicapped children but there was growing interest in and provision for the different types of educationally backward and mentally handicapped children. Educationists were beginning to realise just how much environmental factors could cripple a child's intelligence.

3 and 4. A movable school for gipsy children and a floating school for children of canal workers. Then, it was accepted that schools and teachers should follow the nomads. Nowadays the tendency is to try to persuade them to settle in one place and attend a permanent school.

# Teacher training comes under fire

Insistent questioning of the system of teacher-training led to little real change. The pupil-teacher system finally vanished. LEAs extended their bursary system for intending teachers to university places. But the split between elementary and secondary teacher-training and the gulf between training colleges and universities persisted. A move to bring them together was started by a Departmental Committee Report to the Board of Education in 1925. Its modest proposal was that the Board should cease to examine training college students. The responsibility was given to Joint Boards representing the colleges and the universities in each area. In only a few cases did this mean any extensive co-operation between university and colleges.

The 1925 Report was a disappointment to the NUT. Two Union members of the committee, Miss E. R. Conway and F. J. Sainsbury, signed a Memorandum of Dissent which recommended that all training courses should be post-academic, preferably post-graduate and strictly professional in content. The McNair Report in 1943 went some way towards the ideal of a unified graduate profession, but it is an ideal still to be realised.

5. Social life in the students' hostel at Langham Tower training college, in Sunderland. Sunderland Education Committee established the college in 1908, for men and women. In 1922, when it moved to Langham Tower, it was restricted to women students; in 1970, as the Sunderland College of Education, it again includes men amongst its 700 students.

6. Refresher courses for serving teachers began to be accepted as a very useful feature of the educational scene. These teachers, gathered in the Roman Amphitheatre at Caerleon in 1935, were attending the first course ever to be held in Monmouthshire.

5

6

# World War II

The effects of the Second World War followed the same pattern as the First, but to a heightened degree. Plans for reform at the beginning of the war were abandoned, severe disruption of the schools threw their short-comings into sharp relief, and out of the holocaust came the 1944 Act.

In September 1939, Union headquarters were transferred to Toddington Manor, in Gloucestershire. The following period was one of the most strenuous in the Union's history. The NUT co-operated with the Board and the LEAs to keep education going and the war set the seal on the partnership between the teachers and the two branches of the administration.

The Union was determined not to make the same mistake as in the First War, and pressed for a war bonus as soon as the cost of living began to rise sharply. Several were granted, but the Union had to resort to the National Arbitration Tribunal to make all authorities pay out. The NUT also made strenuous efforts to protect the interests of teachers serving in the armed forces.

1 and 2. Evacuation was an enormous upheaval for children and schools. In an apparently simple plan, the country was divided into evacuated areas, neutral areas and receiving areas. In the first all schools were closed, in the second schools remained normal, in the third schools were expanded to take the extra pupils. The actual process of evacuating nearly a million and a half people went smoothly, but the aftermath was chaotic. The influx of extra pupils showed just how inadequate country schools were; many were still unreorganized all-age schools. Evacuation took the lid off the appalling social conditions in which many slum children were being brought up. The role of the teachers in this fraught situation was vital. Since very few parents stayed with the evacuated children, teachers were the only source of continuity and discipline. H. C. Dent in his account of evacuation in *Education in Transition* describes their efforts as 'superhuman'.

3. A clergyman running an informal school in St Mary's Church, Quarry Hill, Leeds, for children left behind. Evacuation was never made compulsory and as many as a quarter of the children stayed behind or returned. They found schools taken over for other purposes and teachers gone with the evacuees. Where no provision was made for them, there were reports of children running riot – an interesting commentary on the importance of schools in maintaining social order in the towns.

4. Hitler's bombers, naturally enough, did not respect the government's neat division into safe and unsafe areas. The provision of shelters and gasmasks was a further strain on financial and administrative resources.

5. Offers were received from families in the Dominions and the USA to take in British children for the duration of the war. These children were the first batch of nearly 500 to be evacuated to Australia in August 1940. But the idea came to a sad end a month later when the *City of Benares* carrying evacuated children was torpedoed. Only six children survived.

6. A devastated schoolroom in Catford after a direct bomb hit. Thirty children and four teachers were killed.

# The Union shows fighting spirit

A Union stands or falls for the majority of its members by its ability to improve their salaries and conditions of work and to safeguard and promote their interests and welfare. On this basis (although there are often periods when some of the younger or more militant members think that the leadership is reluctant to consider industrial action in support of their demands for improved salaries), the NUT has rarely failed its members. Over the past 50 years, it has fought vigorously to uphold its members' interests, and the Union's mettle was demonstrated convincingly to the Government, education authorities and parents on at least four major occasions.

## The early 1920's

Shortly after the Burnham Committee had been established, the management panel approached teachers in 1922 and asked if they would agree to a 'voluntary' reduction of 5 per cent in their salaries during 1923–24. A special conference of the Union decided reluctantly to accept the cut rather than see the imposition of a more drastic compulsory reduction.

Yet, although it commended the 'public spirited' action of the teachers, the Burnham Committee nevertheless decided that it would make no intervention if authorities refused to pay the agreed scales. Any disputes, it decided, should be settled locally. Supported by this refusal, several authorities tried to lower salaries, and in 1923 the NUT Executive, acting in defence of the newly-established national salary scales, decided that no cut should be accepted which brought any teacher below his correct position on the scale. Unless it acted quickly, the Union thought, other authorities would be tempted to follow suit and Burnham would be eroded. Action was taken and a challenge made to authorities in several areas, notably in Lowestoft, Southampton, Gateshead and South Wales. Schools were closed for 14 weeks in Southampton, for 10 weeks in Gateshead and for 11 months in Lowestoft, where 167 teachers on strike were sustained by the NUT at a cost of about £44,000.

The Lowestoft affair is a good example of the NUT in action during the 1920's. Against the 5 per cent cut that the teachers had accepted, albeit reluctantly, Lowestoft proposed a 10 per cent cut, which the NUT saw as a repudiation of the Burnham Committee scales, a national agreement, and the principle of collective bargaining. The education committee started dismissing its teachers. Acting together, all 167 members of the Union accepted notices terminating their employment. The chairman of the education committee proclaimed his ambition to 'smash' the NUT, as well as the Burnham Com-

mittee. Staff were imported to fill the schools. When the parents of 1600 pupils supported the NUT and refused to send them to school, the authority again got tough. Some of the parents were prosecuted and the authority threatened to withold scholarships from scholarship-holders who were not at school. Meanwhile, the striking teachers opened classes in welfare centres for the children not at school.

The NUT persisted until, eventually, the Board of Education was forced to intervene. It told Lowestoft that its grant was in jeopardy. The warning was followed up by an inspection both of the schools manned by imported labour and the welfare centres. The inspection proved so unfavourable to the schools that the Board withdrew its grant to the Authority. The effect was immediate. Lowestoft established a negotiating committee which met Sir James Yoxall, General Secretary of the NUT, and Fred Mander, his eventual successor; and an agreement, which was highly favourable to the teachers, was reached. Action by the NUT had upheld the newly-established principle of national salary awards.

## The Durham dispute, 1950–52

The Durham dispute started in 1950 when the county council announced its intention to dismiss all employees who were not members of a trade union. Its attempt to implement a closed shop immediately aroused the NUT. Nine out of ten teachers in Durham were members of the NUT but it did not want the authority's help in recruiting still more. The view of the Union was that, although every teacher should belong to a trade union or professional organisation, membership should be a voluntary act by a free individual, exercising his choice without any pressure from his employer. So the Union's 5,000 members in Durham were advised to refuse to disclose whether they were members of a trade union or professional organisation, and the authority was powerless. Although it had lost the first round, Durham did not retire. It started interrogating applicants for teaching posts about their membership of a union. Again the Union acted firmly. The resignations of NUT members in two divisions of Durham were being collected when the Minister issued an order from London that the offending question should not be asked: a second victory for the NUT.

The dispute dragged on for two years. An alliance was formed with doctors, dentists, nurses and engineers in a Joint Committee of the Professions but their case was still subjected by County Hall, according to *The Schoolmaster*, to 'insult, provocation and misrepresentation'. Stronger action became necessary when the authority insisted that

applications for sick pay should be submitted through a professional organisation. All 5,000 teachers in Durham would resign their posts, the NUT then declared, unless the authority retreated. It collected all their resignations which, if posted, would have meant a collapse of the education service in Durham. At the same time, the Union complained to George Tomlinson, Minister of Education, that Durham was exercising its powers unreasonably. Shortly afterwards, Mr Tomlinson wrote to Durham, formally instructing the authority that teachers should not be coerced into union membership. The dispute ended in June 1952 when an arbitration tribunal reported in favour of the NUT. The decision convincingly demonstrated that the numerical strength of the NUT meant power.

Speaking of the Durham dispute to the NUT Conference, Sir Ronald Gould, General Secretary, drew the moral: 'The story of their fight' he said, 'has reverberated round the world and won the admiration of millions. Theirs' was indeed a famous victory, which established not only professional liberty for themselves, but proved a salutary warning to petty tyrants elsewhere who, had it not been for Durham, might have considered tampering with the liberty of the teacher'.

## The fight over pensions, 1954

A spontaneous surge of anger swept through the NUT when Miss Florence Horsbrugh, Minister of Education, asked teachers to accept an increase in their contributions to the Pension Fund from five to six per cent to cover a deficit in the Superannuation Fund. The demand was immediately described by the NUT as equivalent to a cut of one per cent in salaries. Other grounds for the militant – and partly successful – agitation that followed were:

1. Superannuation for teachers was originally intended to be on a non-contributory basis. It became contributory only after the 1925 Superannuation Act which forced teachers to contribute to a pension scheme. They had never agreed with the Contribution and had always considered it as a breach of faith by the Government.

2. Several other Superannuation Funds were in deficit, but had not been singled out, like the teachers, by the Government Actuary.

3. The NUT had campaigned for a pension scheme including provisions for widows and orphans, and was prepared to pay more for the extra benefits – but local authorities had consistently refused to consider such a scheme, or to carry part of its cost. The NUT was not prepared to negotiate with the Government simply on the basis of paying more, but getting nothing in return.

The Union strenuously opposed the Bill

introduced by Miss Horsbrugh. Its campaign was supported by the Opposition, the Liberals and even a few Conservative MPs. As a result of the opposition, the Cabinet decided that the Bill could not be taken through Parliament before July 1, 1954, when it was due to be introduced. Meanwhile, Miss Horsbrugh was replaced by Sir David Eccles, but the Government still said that the Bill would go through before March 1955, but the opposition produced its effect. It took Sir David until October 1955 to finish his discussions with teachers and education authorities. He then announced that the Government would meet the existing deficit (a concession), but added that the contribution was still to be raised to six per cent, and that he was not prepared to endorse a scheme for widows and orphans against the opposition of the education authorities.

The new bill was fought in the country and in parliament, although without the support of teachers in the unions representing the grammar schools. Nearly all the Union's 681 local associations called special protest meetings, at which attendances often jumped up to 80 per cent of the local membership. At a pound a head, the Hertfordshire association collected £1,000 within a month to establish a fighting fund. Schools had played a big part in building up the National Savings Movement and about 27,250 schools had savings groups involving more than two million children, so at this stage the Union decided on a new tactic. It took the unprecedented step of asking all members to stop collecting school savings, although it refused to join the National Association of Schoolmasters in stopping the collection of dinner money.

Again, the opposition of the NUT led to a concession, and in February, 1956, the Government postponed the date of the proposed increase to October 1. It hoped that by then the Burnham Committee would have reached a new salary settlement, which would cancel out the effect of the increased pension contribution. After a two year struggle, the dispute ended when teachers won a salary award raising the basic scale for men from £475 to £900. The award was also coupled with the momentous breakthrough that the scale for women was to rise by yearly increments to full equality with the scale for men by 1961. After 30 years, equal pay for women had been established, but the response from the National Association of Schoolmasters was to appeal to local authorities to refuse it. Equal pay, the Association said, would increase the rates. Only 200 out of 2,000 delegates attending a special conference voted against acceptance of the award, in spite of several reservations, particularly about discrimination against primary school teachers, an issue that was to rankle with the NUT until it next resorted to industrial action in 1967.

**School meals supervision and unqualified teachers, 1967**

Supervising school meals had annoyed teachers for years. It first appeared on the agenda of the NUT Conference in 1948, and by 1965 it was being debated as a subject for industrial action.

Two years later, after expressing its 'deep resentment' at the response to the Union's demand for relief from compulsory dinner duty, the Scarborough conference set up an ad-hoc committee with full powers to plan a phased withdrawal from school meals supervision and to plan sanctions against unqualified teachers.

They were issues on which the rank and file membership were obviously prepared to act. After the ad-hoc committee had made a survey of 627 local associations, which showed that 543 supported action on school meals and 594 on unqualified persons, a referendum in 48 areas gave a vote of about 22,000 out of 31,400 for going ahead with the sanctions. Action involving 8,000 teachers in 18 areas was planned for the autumn with the

The 1961 Burnham settlement did not match teachers' hopes. Some of them wait outside the House of Commons to lobby MPs and others display protest posters outside Hamilton House.

objectives of improving the basic salary scale, obtaining a removal of the primary-secondary differential in salaries, and ending school meals supervision and the employment of unqualified persons.

Once under way, the sanctions won massive support from members in the areas concerned. Although negotiations were going on continuously with the Government and the local authority associations, the Union held referenda in another 17 areas, and decided to extend the sanctions to six new areas in November. Yet before they started, an agreement was reached with the local authorities, under which it was agreed to set up individual working parties to review the primary-secondary differential, to agree on a withdrawal of the clause empowering education authorities to compel teachers to supervise meals, and to study the employment of unqualified persons.

On all of its objectives, except the first, the Union succeeded. The Burnham salary agreement of 1969 improved the number of special allowances in primary schools by 6,000. The obligation on teachers to supervise meals was removed by the Government when the working party reported; and Mr Edward Short, Secretary of State for Education and Science and a life-long member of the NUT, announced in 1969 that after 1970 no unqualified teachers would be employed in schools. He added, moreover, that all graduates would be required to go through a year's training, and that the period of probation for graduates was to be extended to two years instead of one.

Such were four of the battles of the NUT during the past 50 years. Any union, however, is continuously engaged on a variety of fronts. Some may seem insignificant and unexciting by comparison, but all are crucial to the members, or the section of the education service concerned, and help them to feel that a big and powerful Union in London, engaged continually in confrontations with Ministers and civil servants, still belongs intimately to them. A survey of the Union's annual report for 1968, as the NUT approached its centenary, shows some of the areas in which the Union was actively concerned.

The Law and Tenure department, for example, recovered more than £26,000 on behalf of members in compensation for personal injuries. It approved full legal assistance for the next of kin of members who died in the Aberfan disaster, and obtained substantial settlements for them. It was also concerned with civic rights and removing restrictions preventing teachers from participating in local government, with the Offices, Shops and Railway Premises Act, with the closed shop issue in three areas, with residential qualifications in Wales, the tenure of married women teachers, confidential reports by Inspectors, the Code of Professional Conduct, and the scale of fines for assault and non-attendance proceedings.

The Education department had ranged over the following subjects: The Schools Council (and all its committees), Supply and Training of Teachers (including the government of colleges of education, the employment of unqualified persons, teaching practice, in-service training, degrees, student grants and staffing in crisis areas), examinations, ancillary helpers, primary education (including the Plowden Report, parent-teacher relations, and corporal punishment), school meals and milk, the public schools Commission, the youth service, the social services, cuts in educational expenditure, special education, civil defence, school terms and holidays, married women returners, the employment of school children, teacher representation, the treatment of violent refractory children, decimal currency, middle schools, the Industrial Training Act, the migration of children at secondary school stage, the comprehensive school, and absenteeism and delinquency.

Other subjects that it had discussed included: road safety, Union representation on television education committees, distribution of gift packs by teachers, size of classes, liability for pupils visiting industry, levies on library books, draft DES documents, training in driving for children at school, the Open University, purchase tax on mathematical apparatus, and ad-hoc committee on raising the school-leaving age, and fees for classes in leisure time activities.

Apart from an unprecedented level of activity in support of the Union's sanctions on school meals supervision, the Publicity and Public Relations department had organised four regional conferences on The School of the Future, seven public meetings on the Plowden Report, sponsored the Young Film Makers Competition and the fourth national Careers Convention. It had also issued Union publications ranging from 'Education of the Immigrant' and 'Teacher Training' to its booklet, 'University and College Entrance', and 'Teachers and Probation', and had published 550,000 copies of the pamphlet, 'Why Teachers' Pay matters to You and Your Children', and 150,000 copies of a pamphlet on the salaries campaign, apart from all its day-to-day work of press releases and answering inquiries from newspapers.

It had been another busy year for the NUT.

Apart from the action over the supervision of school meals in 1967, the Union by 1969 had initiated no widespread action on any scale in defence of its members' interests since the 1930s. Among the rank and file membership, however, salaries were becoming an increasingly angry issue, and, against initial opposition from the Executive, delegates at the annual conference in Douglas, Isle of Man, carried a resolution calling for the submission of an interim salary claim. Although the Union had only that month signed a new two-year salary agreement, raising the basic scale to £860 to £1,600 over 14 years, the delegates called for an interim increase in April, 1970. They added, moreover, that the Executive was to submit a claim for a ten-year scale of £1,000 to £2,000 for the 1971 settlement.

At the time of the debate, the Government's incomes policy was still operating, allegedly imposing a strict limit of 3½ per cent on all salary increases. Yet, even as the Conference met, BOAC pilots, after striking, were given a settlement well beyond the limit; and as the months followed several groups, including notably dustmen and miners, won increases which seriously breached the official policy. An indication of the resentment that was sweeping through the profession was given during the summer term when an unprecedented number of Inner London teachers called a half-day strike and marched in a procession a mile long to County Hall and on to Westminster. The march was a powerful indication to the Executive that the membership meant business.

Over the summer holiday, the Executive decided to submit a claim for a flat-rate increase of £135 a year, a ten per cent rise which would cost £44m, to restore the salaries of teachers to their July, 1967, level. Once the size of the claim had been agreed, the Union leadership entered into the campaign enthusiastically and it was launched with the unprecedented insertion of full-page advertisements in The Times and The Guardian, stating: "Full-time teacher wanted: starting salary £13 a week", a reference to the take-home pay of many young teachers, drawn up by the Union's vigorous Publicity department.

At the meeting of the Burnham Committee, however, the management panel offered teachers an increase of only £50 a year. At a hurriedly-summoned meeting that night, the Executive unanimously approved plans for strike action on both a local and a national basis, and the first followed the next day and there were several more in the same week, when teachers staged half-day strikes. The action that followed, unprecedented in the history both of the Union and of the state education system, took two forms. One was small-scale action, one or half-day strikes, which were supported by more than 150,000 Union members in the month following the meeting of the Burnham Committee. The second was two-week strikes, supported by 4,000 members (after 5,000 schools had volunteered their support) in 249 schools, action taken jointly with the NAS, whose members struck in 77 schools. It was the first occasion on which the Union had started strike action on anything approaching a national basis, and the effect, once the teachers had shown their strength, was swift.

Any historian has to end his story somewhere, even when the events he is describing are still continuing and unresolved. At the end of December, 1969, however, the militant campaign was showing results. Newspaper polls showed that teachers were supported by parents. The Secretary of State for Education and Science declared his own sympathy. Many MPs rallied in support of the teachers, and editorials in the newspapers almost unanimously supported the salaries campaign. So much support was forthcoming, even from leaders of education authorities, that the management panel was about to make a new offer of up to £85. It was not going to be good enough for the NUT and it was preparing still further two-week strikes at the start of 1970. As it approached its centenary, it was returning to the militant traditions on which it was founded in 1870. Its membership was roused as it had not been for 50 years, and it looked as though it would get the results that rewarded the similar efforts of its founders a century before.

# Free secondary education – for all
## *1944 Act*

The 1944 Education Act – the famous 'Butler Act' – was an end and a beginning: the end of more than ten years of controversy over the future shape of the education service, and the beginning of an era of reform and expansion which still continues. The Act set up a new Ministry of Education with increased powers and divided the whole State system into three parts – primary, secondary and further education. All children were now to be educated in separate secondary schools after the age of 11; grammar school fees, except in direct grant schools, were to be abolished; the school leaving age was to go up to 16, although no date was fixed for this; and for the 16–18 age group there were to be county colleges for further training. The Act was welcomed by the teachers for, as Sir Frederick Mander, general secretary of the NUT commented, it removed the word elementary, and with it a badge of inferiority, from British education.

1. The 'all-age' elementary school had catered for children from 5 to 14, and the Act of 1944 sounded its death knell. But it was a long time dying and in 1967 there were still 71 'all-age' schools catering for about 16,000 children, most of them in rural areas.

2. For most children the break in schooling at 11 meant an examination or test, soon to become famous as the Eleven Plus. The 1944 Act did not make a tripartite system of secondary education mandatory, but most education authorities decided to divide children between grammar, secondary modern and, in some areas, technical schools. The number of grammar school places varied from 10.5 per cent to 45 per cent from area to area.

3. Few technical schools were ever built and in most areas the Eleven Plus was a choice between the existing grammar schools or the new secondary modern schools, many of which were converted elementary schools. But as money became available new secondary modern schools were built – this one at Tooting was the LCC's first post-war secondary building and cost £56,000.

# The religious issue

One of the fiercest controversies leading up to the 1944 Act was that over religious education and the role of the churches in the schools. The NUT bitterly opposed church interference with, or inspection of religious education classes or any test of the religious beliefs of teachers. In the event, the Act included a 'conscience clause' for teachers, who were not to be penalised in any way for their religious opinions, or lack of them, nor compelled to give religious instruction. R.E. was to be Christian but non-denominational in the local authority schools, and to be taught according to an agreed syllabus worked out by the teachers, the churches and the local authorities together.

1

2

1. Prayers had traditionally been part of the school day and the 1944 Act made a daily act of worship obligatory. Parents retained the right to withdraw their children on conscientious grounds.

2. The only 'compulsory' school subject – religious education. In most schools the Christian year starts with the traditional nativity play.

3. The voluntary schools – originally founded by the religious denominations – retained their semi-independent status under the Act. About one-third of all schools now have voluntary status and the amount of freedom they have in giving denominational instruction varies according to the amount of public money they receive. About 8,000 are run by the Church of England, 2,000 by the Roman Catholic Church and a couple of hundred by other denominations.

3

# The outsiders

The 1944 Act demanded provision for many of the children previously thought to be outside the scope of the education service. Nursery education was to be encouraged, although not made obligatory, because the Act dealt only with children over five, and education was to be provided for school-age children with any kind of handicap, physical or mental. Local authorities were also made responsible for finding out how many children in their area required treatment and were obliged to examine children to find out their needs. Teaching had to be provided for the blind, partially sighted, deaf, partially hearing, delicate, educationally subnormal, epileptic, maladjusted, physically handicapped and those with speech defects.

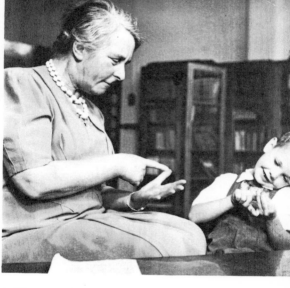

6

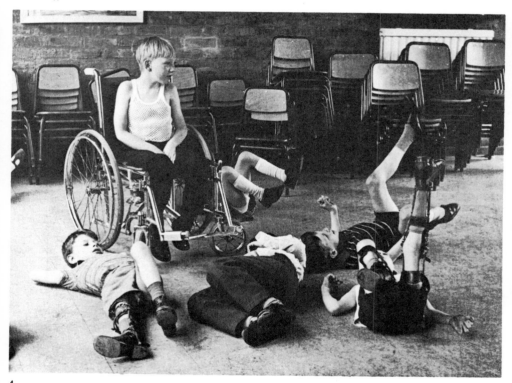

4

5

4. There are about 74,000 children in special schools, many of them residential. Attendance is compulsory until the age of 16 and some schools keep children longer for further education and training. The schools are run by the local authorities and by voluntary organisations.

5. Expansion of nursery education, although suggested by the 1944 Act, has been held back by successive financial crises and by the shortage of teachers. Local authorities have concentrated resources on provision for school-age children and permission for the building of nursery classes or schools has been almost impossible to obtain since the Act.

6. Since the Act it has been found possible to help other types of handicapped child for whom no previous provision was made – there are new schools for spastic children, like this little boy learning to form his words, and for aphasic, dyslexic and autistic children.

# Opportunity

After 1944, the efforts of the NUT were devoted to ensuring that the promise of Secondary Education for All, the vision of the Hadow Report which was now enshrined in the new Act, was fulfilled. Nor was the let-down so rapid as it had been after 1918. The school-leaving age was raised to 15 in 1947, and the laborious process of reorganising secondary education was got in hand. Yet the Union still had an agenda of new reforms. One was equal pay for women, on which it persisted until victory was achieved in the mid-1950s (and which is described elsewhere). It was also fighting for the money needed to implement all the provisions of the new Act. It was concerned about the duty of supervising school meals, about parity of esteem for primary and secondary schools, about school building, about the size of classes and the different limits set for primary and secondary schools, and especially about professional status.

On all these issues, the agitation continued throughout the next 20 years, but already there were early signs of the untapped potential that was now being brought to light as a result of the new act, and which was ironically to delay some of the progress in implementing it. Mr I. Gwynne Rees, president of the NUT in 1949, reported a 35 per cent increase in School Certificate and a 90 per cent increase in Higher School Certificate passes compared with 1938. There were 66 per cent more teachers at training colleges, state scholarships and awards for further education had doubled, and the school building programme for 1949 was £55m compared with £23m in 1948. The NUT, however, was already detecting the issue which was to become paramount by the 1960s. Unless primary schools were given a better deal, Mr Rees argued, the gap between the gifted and the less gifted would grow still wider. At the same conference, an indication of the preoccupations of the Union were given when delegates passed a resolution appealing for a more rapid implementation of the 1944 Act, a substantial increase in school and college building, priority for primary schools, a rapid expansion of permanent facilities for teacher training, immediate implementation of recommendations on university awards as a step towards university admission by merit only, a withdrawal of the ban on nursery school development, and an expansion of higher technical education.

It was not long, however, before the familiar pattern re-established itself. The early 1950s saw the country once again faced with the need for economy. It was the period of the cold war. Money was being poured into defence and the terrible twins – the trend and the bulge – made their first appearance on the educational stage. The bulge was the steep rise in the birthrate after the war, which meant not only new schools but also new houses. As Mr A. Granville Prior, NUT president in 1951, pointed out, it also meant that the education budget could afford no luxuries, only the bare necessities. More than 1,100,000 school places had to be built between 1947–53 solely to put roofs over children's heads. The trend, which made its real appearance somewhat later, was the increasing tendency for more pupils to stay at school beyond the minimum leaving age; one of the hopes, of course, of the 1944 Act, but which when fulfilled raised costs. Although the size of the education budget increased relentlessly, it was increasing simply to stand still, and it meant that many of the features of the new Act, the idea of County Colleges in particular, were delayed or never implemented.

As usual, teachers acknowledged that progress was being made, but argued that it was not fast enough. A decade after the Act had been passed, during the years 1955, 1956 and 1957, three successive presidents, Herbert Nursey, Edward Britton (eventual successor to Sir Ronald Gould as General Secretary), and John Archbold, summed up the mood of the Union and defined its new commitments.

Nursey argued that teachers could be proud of their results since 1944. Twice as many students were going to university, successes at the GCE, now at a higher academic standard, were mounting, the curriculum had been broadened, and the secondary modern schools were doing valiant work. In 1954, 24,000 pupils at them had opted to stay on after 15 and 5,500 had sat the GCE. More than 2,000 new primary schools and over 600 new secondary schools had been built. There were 80,000 extra teachers and 380,000 young men and women were on part-time day release – but nearly half the children were still in oversize classes.

Yet Britton pointed out that the forces of ignorance, apathy and self-complacency were still rampant, and that the successes had been achieved at the price of heroic work by teachers. Steadily and inescapably, conditions had deteriorated, he declared.

'Wages have declined in value until each one of us can look round and see unskilled and socially unimportant jobs being better paid; the actual classroom work of teaching has steadily become more exacting and more exhausting, and duties outside the classroom have become more oppressive; and, in spite of many new school buildings, taking the field as a whole, the conditions of overcrowding and inadequate provision have become steadily worse. People outside the schools talk about the past ten years as a period of great educational advance. In a sense they are right. The school-leaving age has been raised; the vastly increased numbers of children have all been found places at school, and much progress has been made towards reorganisation of full-range schools into primary and secondary schools. But only those who work in the schools know how much of that progress has depended on teachers' self-sacrifice, teachers' improvisations, and teachers' willingness to accept more onerous conditions of work for the sake of better educational opportunity for the child. But the teachers know, and the teachers look around and see that all the thanks they have received have been a steadily declining standard of living and a succession of ill-informed canards in press and public platform blaming the profession for juvenile delinquency, juvenile illiteracy, juvenile indiscipline, and all the other ills the times are heir to. It is hardly surprising that this mounting sense of frustration should have shown itself in angry meetings, angry public protest and in talk of sanctions'.

Out of the contemplation on the decade since 1944 and the resolutions that were persistently debated at annual conferences, three major pre-occupations for the Union emerged: an improvement in the professional status of the teacher, an 'onslaught' on school building conditions, and a refinement of the concept of equality of opportunity. Britton argued that the Union and the education service should already be planning for the year, 2,000, and both Nursey and Archbold suggested that the Government's priorities should be to arrest early leaving, an alleviation of the defects suffered by children because of social conditions, increased maintenance allowances for pupils of 15 plus, an attack on overcrowded schools and oversize classes, and the institution of three-year training for all teachers.

The status of teachers was a personal preoccupation of Sir Ronald Gould and it had been a frequent theme of his annual addresses to Conference. It now became one of the principal issues of the NUT. At the 1954 Conference, Gould had outlined five aims: only trained teachers should be allowed to teach, qualifications should not be easily achieved, salaries and conditions of work should be improved, teachers should unite, and they should act professionally as individuals. A year later he returned to the same theme and appealed to Lord Hailsham to name an early date for the institution of three-year training. His timing was opportune. Seven thousand extra teachers a year were being produced by the training colleges, and the staffing position was improving. The peak of the bulge was nearly through the schools. Yet if school rolls were dropping some authorities might be tempted to start skimping on teachers. Three-year training would also stop any threat of unemployment.

On this occasion, Sir Ronald outlined a three-fold strategy: a three-year course, training for all new entrants, and the elimination of all unqualified teachers. A degree of ruthlessness was necessary, he said, if teachers were to achieve professional status. *'To being with, there must be more rigorous selection of students on entry. We must demand higher academic standards: exceptional entry should be reserved for the really exceptional. Then, the content of the courses must be improved. The three-year course will fail us if it degenerates into a two year course at a slower pace. The academic standard should be high. Every student should study one or more subjects to degree standard. Again, the standard required at the end of the course must be stepped up . . . It is our duty to aim at standards for the teaching profession as high as for other professions. After that, it will be ludicrous to leave unchanged the position of untrained teachers, and the door should be barred to any future entrants of this kind. Our profession has been wide open to archaeologists, linguists, physicists, chemists, doctors, dentists, lawyers and musicians. We have admitted them all with teacher training. We must bar the door to them unless they take at least one year's training as teachers. If we did this at the same time as establishing the three-year course, teachers' qualifications would be reduced to a much simpler pattern. All new entrants would be trained and all would have some claim to scholarship'.*

The appeal was answered only a few years later, and the three-year course started in September 1960. The two other strands of the strategy had to wait until a member of the NUT, Mr Edward Short, was Secretary of State for Education and Science, until once again there was a threat of unemployment amongst teachers, and, in one instance, until the NUT took industrial action in 1967. Unqualified teachers will no longer be employed in schools after 1970, mainly because of the NUT sanctions, and Mr Short announced in 1969 that all graduates were to undergo in future a two, instead of a one year, period of probation, or to hold a Diploma in Education.

On school building conditions, the NUT was as good as its word. It mounted a relentless lobby for improvements, which culminated in the Campaign for Educational Advance in 1963. A survey by the Executive in 1958 had disclosed what Miss A. F. Cooke, the president, described as a 'pitiful' story of appalling school conditions. A £300m school building programme over five years had been promised, but it was still not enough, she warned, to deal with schools with bucket sanitation, or without electric light, storage space, cloakrooms, or rooms for the staff and the head.

The crucial onslaught followed the publication in 1963 of the Union's publication, *The State of Our Schools*, describing a survey of conditions in more than 22,000 schools during 1962. The disclosures from it were put across to the public in a major publicity exercise which was followed by the Campaign. Again, the story seemed pitiful.

One in two primary schools dated from the 19th century. One in five were overcrowded. Two out of five had outside lavatories.

Seventeen per cent had no hot water. More than 40 per cent had no staff room. Two out of three secondary modern schools were overcrowded and more than half needed specialist teachers for backward children. More than half the grammar schools were overcrowded and one in five was without stage facilities, separate dining rooms, or a gymnasium. A 17 per cent annual turnover

A press conference following Burnham negotiations. Sir Ronald Gould answers reporters' questions.

among women teachers was disclosed and an urgent need for more science and mathematics teachers, amounting to 28 per 100 schools in mathematics.

Two years later, the Government, after a long delay, published a report on its own survey of school building standards, also made in 1962. It supported the results of the NUT survey and helped to underline them. Two million children were spending their formative years in severely sub-standard buildings and 500,000 were still dining in their classrooms. There were 17,200 schools with mainly outdoor sanitation, 8,800 without staffrooms, 7,500 dating from before 1875 and 15,200 from before 1902. The report estimated that it would cost £1,368m to bring all buildings up to contemporary standards.

Equality of opportunity, a cause that the Union had espoused since 1919, had been the objective of the Butler Act, and some progress had certainly been made towards its fulfilment. There was more equality of opportunity in the 1950s than in the 1930s, but it was being taken mostly by the middle classes, and huge pockets of deprivation still persisted. After 1954, however, sociological studies and a series of major reports from the Central Advisory Council on Education, (CAC) under Lord Crowther, Sir John Newsom and Lady Plowden, coupled with the report on Higher Education from a Committee under Lord Robbins, started to show the inequalities that still persisted below the surface of an increasingly affluent Britain, and to champion the cause of the underprivileged.

The first report to show the influence of social class on academic performance was *Early Leaving*, published by the CAC (of which Sir Ronald Gould was a member), in 1954. It recommended improved main-

tenance allowances for deprived children staying on at school beyond 15, as well as legislation for the payment of family allowances in respect of all children still at school, two reforms that had been advocated constantly by the NUT.

Yet the series of major documents which collectively presented a powerful indictment of the inequalities that still persisted even in 1969 and which were to form the agenda for the preparation of the next major act, started with the Crowther Report in 1959. Set up to consider the education of boys and girls between 15 and 18, the Crowther Council showed that only 12 per cent of the 17 year olds and six per cent of the 20 year old age groups were still in full-time education. It criticised the waste of potential that the country was tolerating, recommended the raising of the school-leaving age to 16 between 1966 and 1968 and the introduction of County Colleges early in the 1970s. It also advocated a 20-year programme to ensure that by 1980 half the boys and girls in the country should be in full-time education until 18. Using the new evidence from sociological studies, it suggested that early leaving was a social rather than an academic phenomenon, and demonstrated that many pupils failed to fulfil their academic potential because of the social limitations of their family backgrounds. Its philosophy, which was to be restated and refined in all the succeeding reports, was expressed early in the Report:

*'This report is about the education of English boys and girls aged from 15 to 18. Most of them are not being educated. But they are all at a highly impressionable age, with their characters still being formed, and, except in rare instances, with their minds still capable of considerable development. It seems to us clear that it is both necessary and practicable greatly to extend in the next few years the provision made for boys and girls in their later teens . . . We could not as a nation enjoy the standard of living we have today on the education we gave our children a hundred or even 50 years ago. If we are to build a higher standard of living, and – what is more important – if we are to have higher standards of life, we shall need a firmer educational base than we have today. Materially and morally, we are compelled to go forward'.*

The next brief to the CAC, now under Sir John Newsom, was to consider the education between 13 and 16 of pupils of average or less than average ability. The Newsom Council reported in 1963 and followed Crowther, as well as the principal recommendation made to it by the NUT, in recommending the raising of the school leaving age to 16. It showed that four out of five schools for Newsom children (as they came to be known), were seriously deficient.

Sir Ronald Gould addressing the conference of the World Confederation of Organisations of the Teaching Profession, of which he is president.

Schools for Newsom children, moreover, got less than their fair share of resources and more than their fair share of the least well-qualified teachers. It also followed Crowther in suggesting that many children were being held back more by social than genetic factors, although school standards were rising sharply. Another recommendation, which was to be expanded in the Plowden Report, was that a joint working party should be set up on Social Services in Slum Areas. Yet another, demonstrating that the NUT 'onslaught' was bearing fruit, called for accelerated action to remedy the 'functional deficiencies' of the schools.

Above all, however, the report pleaded for a change of heart towards the pupils whose education it was considering. 'Our concern', it said, 'is lest the relatively unspectacular needs of the boys and girls with whom we are concerned should be overlooked. They have had far more than their share of thoroughly unsatisfactory buildings and desperately unsettling changes of staff. Given the opportunities, we have no doubt that they will rise to the challenge which a rapidly developing economy offers no less to them than to their abler brothers and sisters. But there is no time to waste. Half our future is in their hands. We must see that it is in good hands'.

Yet apart from its own recommendations, the Newsom Report was the occasion for a momentous breakthrough in official thinking and in the definition of equality of opportunity. It was heralded in the foreword to the report written by Sir Edward Boyle, Minister of Education. One of the most significant movements of the past 25 years, Sir Ronald Gould now thinks, was the swing in educational philosophy from its belief in pre-destination, or that all children are born with fixed abilities, to a belief in salvation, or that nurture is as crucial as nature. The first

official breakthrough for the nurture theorists arrived when Sir Edward, writing of the Newsom children, said: 'Their potentialities are no less real, and of no less importance, because they do not readily lend themselves to measurement by the conventional critieria of academic achievement. The essential point is that all children should have an equal opportunity of *acquiring* intelligence and of

Sir Geoffrey Crowther, who chaired the committee which reported on the education of boys and girls between 15 and 18.

developing their talents and abilities to the full'.

Updating the concept of equality of opportunity had so far covered the 15 to 18 and the 13 to 16 age ranges. Attention then turned to the over 18s and to higher education. The NUT, in its evidence to the Robbins Committee, said that one thing was certain. The theory of a more or less fixed pool of ability had been proved wrong by the educational developments of the past decade. There was at present a considerable waste of human resources because of the inadequate provision of education in general, and of higher education in particular. It was clear. the Union added, that there was room for expansion without any lowering of standards. It also reiterated its aim of a four-year trained, all-graduate profession. The NUT was not, of course, the only organisation that raised doubts about a fixed pool of ability, but the argument was nevertheless resoundingly championed when the Robbins Committee reported in 1963.

It recommended that by 1980 the percentage of the age group going into higher education should be raised from eight to 17 per cent and that the student population, 216,000 in 1962–63, should expand to 390,000 by 1973 and to 560,000 by 1980 (all of which targets were to be substantially exceeded). Another major recommendation was that responsibility for the Colleges of Education should be transferred to the universities, it also mooted the idea of the Bachelor of Education degree, a reform advocated for years by the NUT, and which was eventually adopted, although the Colleges themselves stayed outside the universities.

The axiom of the Committee, was that higher education should be available for all who were qualified by ability and attainment to pursue it, a significant advance on the old concept of equality of opportunity. Antici-

pating any challenge, the Report also offered a vindication of its recommendations, a vindication which foreshadowed the development of theme Secondary Education for All into the theme for the second century of state education of Higher Education for All. It said: '*Conceiving education as a means, we do not believe that modern societies can achieve their aims of economic growth and higher cultural standards without making the most of the talents of their citizens ... To realise the aspirations of a modern community as regards both wealth and culture, a fully educated population is necessary. But beyond that, education ministers to ultimate ends, in developing man's capacity to understand, to contemplate and to create, and it is characteristic of the aspirations of this age to feel that, where there is capacity to pursue such activities, there that capacity should be fostered. The good society desires equality of opportunity for its citizens to become not merely good producers but also good men and women*'.

It was nevertheless the third major CAC document, the Plowden Report on Children and their Primary Schools, which most significantly shifted the public mood. It appeared at the end of an epoch when most of the attention had been concentrated on secondary schools and university expansion; and when public interest, stimulated by a new generation of young parents who were showing an unprecedented interest in state education, was starting to turn towards the primary schools. It was now 23 years since the last major Education Act and a new Act was being mooted. Above all, there was the cumulative impact of four major reports in eight years. After the stately succession of Crowther, Newsom, Robbins, and Plowden, the next leap forward was irresistible.

The NUT, a union which speaks above all for the primary school, had also been sharpening the public appetite. The question of oversize classes in primary schools was raised by G. A. Chappell in his presidential address in 1961 and at the same conference Sir Ronald Gould, always ahead of official thinking, had proposed five measures to raise the status of the primary school and to prevent a split in the teaching profession. Work in primary schools should be made more attractive financially, he said. The social and educational merits of the primary school should be extolled by teachers and the Government. Training should be made compulsory for all teachers, and training colleges should set their academic standards higher. The public mood, therefore, was obviously ripe for Plowden.

Nine out of ten teachers in primary schools belong to the NUT, and the Union siezed its opportunity to canvass the Council energetically. All of its local associations were invited to help in the preparation of evidence and more than 1,000 comments and answers from replies to a questionnaire went into the document, '*First Things First*', which was submitted to the Council. It was described as a milestone in the Union policy. *First Things First* warned the Plowden Council in particular about the false prophets who would recommend that it should plan a primary school system which could function within the nation's allegedly limited resources. No similar opportunity of stating the needs of the nation's younger children might occur for a very long time, the Union said. It was also likely that parliament would soon need to rewrite the 1944 Act, and the philosophy and content of any new Act would be profoundly influenced by what was said by Crowther, Newsom, Robbins, and in this instance, Plowden.

It went on: 'A study of the major acts of this century shows that they are always programmes of future development rather than statements of aims already attained. The NUT pleads for a consideration of the problems of the primary school that will not merely offer solutions for present difficulties but will boldly outline plans for its future development'. The document made a host of recommendations, including nursery education from three and infant education from the start of the school year in which a child was five, both of which were endorsed and expanded by the Plowden Council. It also anticipated in embryo the major recommendation of the Council, when it proposed special attention for primary schools in the problem areas of big cities and urged that education authorities needed special help if there was to be any equalisation of educational opportunity between areas of unequal development.

Such special priority, in the event, was to form the basis for the major proposal by the Plowden Council – the establishment of educational priority areas (EPAs), coupled with the concept of 'positive discrimination' as a matter of national policy in favour of schools in deprived areas in order the make a reality of equality of opportunity. Now, for the first time, it had been recognised that it was not enough simply to wave some magic Government wand and murmur Equality of Opportunity, and just hope it would occur. The Council also suggested criteria for assessing which areas most needed special help and where educational handicaps were reinforced by social handicaps.

The acceptance of the principle of positive discrimination by the Government, when Mr Crosland, Secretary of State, announced a special £16m building programme to help schools in EPAs, when the Burnham Committee agreed to pay an extra £75 a year to teachers working in them, and when Mr Short sanctioned the first nursery school

Lord and Lady Plowden. Lady Plowden gave her name to the Plowden Report on primary schools.

building programme since the war, and directed it to the EPAs, was perhaps the most significant educational and social advance of the 1960s.

Meanwhile, the Union had not been distracted from its ordinary work. Several important gains for teachers were being consolidated. It was also starting to look forward to its centenary and to look back on what had been achieved since 1870. The next major step for teachers, according to Dame Muriel Stewart, president in 1964, was full professional freedom, and she detected two significant straws in the wind. One was the establishment of the Certificate of Secondary Education, a nationally recognised examination for the 40 per cent of children immediately below and overlapping with the GCE group, and largely meant for secondary modern schools. What was new about the CSE was that teachers were given new professional responsibilities for the examination. There was a majority of teachers, and of the NUT, on the governing councils, its examination committees and its subject panels. The second step forward was the Schools Council, established in 1964, to study and report on the curriculum, teaching methods and examinations, and to stimulate changes. Originally it was greeted with suspicion. Teachers feared that the Ministry was trying to centralise control of the curriculum, but when the Council was established representatives of teachers formed a majority of its 50 members. It also upheld the independence of teachers and the schools for their own work. Dame Muriel Stewart became its second chairman and it was eventually seen by the NUT as one of the most promising new developments of the decade. The way towards two other momentous reforms was also being paved. Sir Edward Boyle had committed the Government to the raising of the school-leaving age to 16 in 1970, and Mr Crosland announced in 1965 that all education authorities were being asked to submit plans to start comprehensive schools, so initiating the move towards universal comprehensive education.

After publication of the Plowden Report in 1967, the need for reforms was widely accepted, only the money to put them into effect was wanting. It was in 1967, ironically, that the aspirations released by the makers of the 1944 Act ran head on into the nation's persistent economic crisis. Spending on education had been increasing at an average rate of about ten per cent a year for twenty years. Suddenly, the Government decided that the country should start living within its means. After a long debate, the Government announced in January 1968 that the raising of the school leaving age was to be postponed for two years, against the overwhelming opposition of the education service, in which the NUT figured prominently. Still worse, in the view of educationists, was the announcement that spending on education was to be limited to annual increases of under four per cent in real terms. Once again, the NUT was in the forefront of the campaign against the drastic economy measures.

The NUT conference in 1968 deplored the postponement of the raising of the school

leaving age, which it declared would deny opportunities to the under-privileged child, threaten the implementation of the Plowden Report, delay the satisfactory reorganisation of secondary education, and restrict the output of better trained and skilled manpower. Sir Ronald Gould declared that the socially under-privileged needed nursery schools, better built and equipped primary schools, better staffing and the raising of the school leaving age even more than the socially well-provided.

'I believe', he said, 'that it is morally and socially indefensible that those living in the impoverished, decaying centre of a city have much poorer opportunities than those living in the lusher, expanding and developing suburbs. I believe that it is morally and socially indefensible that less than a third of children remain at school after 15 in the Northern region compared with more than half in the South East'.

'*I believe that implementing Plowden, Newsom and Crowther would do more for racial harmony than any Race Relations Act, and more for personal satisfaction, social harmony and economic well-being than anything else that could be done by Government or by local authorities*'.

Sir Ronald also outlined what the new limit on spending would mean: the employment of fewer teachers, fewer ancillaries and the sacking of part-time teachers; fewer audio-visual aids, a cut in capitation allowances, a blow to in-service training, and deferment of spending on the maintenance and decoration of schools, as well as of school building itself. Some education authorities were forced to prune their minimum budgets by up to £1m in 1969.

Yet at the 1969 conference, and in his farewell address to the Union, Sir Ronald also vividly underlined the dilemma that the Government and the education service was facing, and which seemed certain to dominate the politics of education over the next decade. Whatever were the intentions of Governments to restrict spending, he pointed out, several factors were exerting an enormous upward thrust on educational spending: the steady democratisation of the education system, the belief that education would strengthen the country socially and economically, the insatiable needs of industry, and the growth of Britain's social conscience. Crowther, he said, had pointed to waste of potential beyond 15, Newsom to the waste of half our future, Robbins to the waste of so much university potential, and Plowden to the waste because of social circumstances. The more people exercised their consciences about the quality of contemporary life, the more they would turn to the education system.

'The history of the past 35 years has shown that once the Government has fixed new objectives, as it did in 1944, there is an insistent demand to reach them. If in 1969 there is a new Education Act with new objectives (say, for example, universal comprehensive education), demands to implement the Act will develop and every step forward will cost money ... Rising aspirations must be accompanied by rising expenditure'.

The economic circumstances that were afflicting the education system were depressing, but the NUT, in common with the rest of the education service, was starting to look towards the year, 2,000, and to think about the new Education Act which was now under active consideration by the Government, and due for the early 1970s. Although its discussion document, *Into the 1970s*, was still proposing some measures that were advocated before 1944, it also took a long look forward, stepped into new areas, and proposed a challenging programme of action for the future. Its introduction was as good a summary as any of what had been achieved since 1870 and what was needed in the next century of education. The nation, it said, was now dependent as never before upon education. Britain today had to maintain its economic existence in a highly competitive and highly industrialised world in which it had few natural resources other than the ability of its people. Living under the shadow of the atom bomb, collectively and individually, economically and spiritually, they were subjected to pressures that would have seemed impossible in 1870. Nor, moreover, was the process at an end. The world of 2,000 AD would be far more complex than the world of 1970 – yet this was the world for which the schools were educating their pupils. So a new Education Act was needed. The state education system, shaped for the needs of the 1940s, was no longer able to meet the demands that would be made on it in the 1970s.

It went on:—

'The education service has developed at an explosive rate since the passing of the 1944 Act. Both quantitatively and qualitatively the growth has been staggering. In 1938–39 education in England and Wales cost £114m. In 1967–68 it was £1,891m. Between 1948 and 1967 the school population increased from 5,356,000 to 7,328,000; and the number of teachers in primary and secondary schools increased from 196,000 to 317,000. Over the same period the number of children over 15 remaining in full-time education rose from 187,000 to 519,000; the number of full-time students in colleges of education rose from 8,500 to 95,000; in further education from 47,000 to 197,000; and in the universities from 78,000 to 199,000. In summer 1953, 183,000 candidates obtained 592,000 passes in G.C.E. 'O' Level; in 1965, 449,000 candidates obtained 1,252,000 passes. In summer, 1953, 45,000 candidates obtained 83,000 passes in G.C.E. 'A' Level; in 1965, 147,000 candidates obtained 291,000 passes. Moreover, although these criteria apply to the upper end of the system, the growth has been of the system as a whole. Development in secondary and higher education cannot take place unless there has been comparable growth of the foundations laid in the primary schools.

'Yet in spite of this growth the outstanding characteristic of the system is its profligate waste of ability. There is waste of ability before the child enters school, waste at 11 +, waste at school leaving age, waste at entry to the sixth form, and waste at university entrance. There is waste of ability in innumerable badly designed, badly equipped and badly staffed schools. The present distribution of educational resources still very often means that the "haves" receive positive discrimination in their favour, while the "have nots" lose even the little that might be theirs. The chances of geography, sex and social class still place considerable barriers in the way of equal opportunity. Boys still have more than twice as much chance of going to university as girls, while children brought up in socially and culturally deprived "twilight areas" of large towns have virtually lost their chance of educational advancement before they reach the secondary school, and probably before they reach school age at all. This has been proved by numerous reports in the past ten years. The pessimists who speak of exhausting the pool of ability and scraping the bottom of the barrel are ignoring the evidence.

'A further point must not be overlooked. The experience of advanced nations, and particularly of America, indicates that with the advance of technology, the uneducated and semi-educated become progressively less employable. There is no future for unskilled labour in a modern society. The typical pattern in an advanced nation is the existence of chronic unemployment among unskilled workers alongside a chronic shortage of labour in all occupations requiring a high standard of education and skill. Moreover, as technology advances, a high degree of skill and a high level of education become more nearly synonymous. Mechanical skills that do not require a high level of education can be performed by the sophisticated machines of modern industry. To plan a future in which an appreciable proportion of the population is at a low level of education is to plan a future in which there will be permanent unemployment. In the past we have been prepared to budget for a society based upon periodic unemployment; to permit young people to grow up with a low level of general education is to budget for a future in which the community will contain a permanent element of both unemployed and unemployable persons.

'Nor is this confined to the economic aspects of existence. The developments of technology have made life incomparably more complex than it used to be. Man today is presented at once with more opportunities and more risks than he ever was. His opportunities for the enjoyment of music and the arts, of foreign travel and an extended leisure are greater than they ever were; yet modern techniques of mass communication and mass persuasion have placed him more completely at the mercy of the propagandist and the demagogue. The quality of his life depends more than ever upon his ability to understand the world in which he lives and the people with whom he lives, and this is only possible if he has a high standard of education.

'The need therefore is for a large growth in educational provision. In England and Wales 70% have left school by the age of 16. By 1985 there should be at least a million full-time students in higher and further education and 10 million children and young people in schools and junior colleges. This is not a luxury to be afforded if we can; it is a necessity without which the economic, social and cultural life of the nation is in jeopardy. Britain is inexorably moving along the path to an educationally based technological society. It is essential that a new education act should lay the philosophic and administrative foundations for a continued and rapid educational growth. The 1944 Act laid such a basis for the past 25 years, but it no longer meets society's needs. A new act is required to meet the challenge of the 1970s'.

Among the proposals that the NUT made were:—

1. As a result of the nature versus nurture argument over IQ, the duty of the parent should be defined as to secure full-time education for the child in an educational institution approved by the Secretary of State (a proposal with significant implications for independent schools).
2. Pupils should be educated in accordance with their parents' wishes so far as is consistent with the pursuit of public policy, so that some parents could not frustrate national educational policy.
3. School entry should be at the beginning of the academic year when children reached the age of five. Compulsory attendance should begin on the September 1st after a child reached his 4th birthday.
4. A duty should be laid on education authorities to provide nursery education from three, and they should be permitted to provide it from two.
5. The school-leaving age should be raised to 16 in 1972.
6. There should be one set of regulations for pupils between 5 and 16.
7. Legislation should be enacted to ensure a universal system of comprehensive education.
8. There should be one set of regulations for all education beyond 16.
9. There should be compulsory day-release to 19, organised by education authorities in consultation with employers.

The Secretary of State for Education and Science, Edward Short, addressing the 1969 NUT conference at Douglas, Isle of Man.

Lord Butler, who piloted the 1944 Act through parliament.

10. Teachers should possess the same freedom over the religious education syllabus as over other parts of the curriculum, but under local religious education advisory committees. The corporate act of worship should not necessarily be at the start of the school day. Religious instruction should be voluntary after 16.

11. The Secretary of State should be given the duty of approving the constitution of education committees, so that they were not emasculated by reforms in local government and to ensure the representation of teachers.

12. Schools should have academic boards so that teachers could get their views heard by the Governors.

The document then went on to discuss higher education, the controversial area where most of the reforms during the next era of educational development seemed certain to occur, especially under the pressure of steeply rising demand. As in 1944 the Union had proposed a unified system of secondary schooling, so in 1970 it recommended a unified system of higher education. An unplanned system, it said, was bound to involve wasteful duplication of expensive equipment and buildings, and an uneconomic use of expert teaching manpower. The colleges of education and the technical colleges could not plan their courses if the university sector of higher education was free to develop what courses it liked, irrespective of what was being done elsewhere. Nor could the total output of students from higher education bear any resemblance to employment prospects if the university sector was not co-ordinated with the other two sectors in considering national needs.

'If the university sector is allowed to develop independently of the rest of the higher education system chance will play too large a part in the composition of the total output of educated manpower for any such certainty to exist. This would be true if the university sector were planned as a whole. When the university sector is composed of 44 separate universities each jealously defending its right to be independent of all the others, chance is allowed to operate to the point of chaos.

'Nor are the harmful effects of the failure to plan as a whole only felt within higher education itself. The effects upon secondary education are in some respects even more serious. The multiplying of different university faculty requirements has become a by-word. There can even be different faculty requirements for the same subject within the same university. In consequence preparation for university entrance imposes an altogether unnecessary and wasteful fractionalisation of sixth form classes upon every secondary school where pupils are seeking university entrance. It imposes a degree of specialisation upon the sixth forms of all schools with pupils seeking university entrance that is altogether harmful and because of the need for the economic use of staff and equipment the same specialisation also has to be imposed upon young people who have no intention of going to a university. Moreover, this domination of secondary school curricula by the universities is now showing signs of preventing the proper development of new courses in the sixth forms that are growing up in secondary schools.

'For these reasons we are convinced that machinery should be created which makes possible the over-all planning of all higher education, including the Open University. The object of this planning should be to avoid the wasteful duplication of courses in higher education both as between university and university and between university and other institutions of higher education; to ensure that the total out-put of students in each specialisation in higher education bears a reasonable resemblance to the prospects of employment for that specialisation, and by co-ordinating the entrance requirements for various courses in higher education to relieve the pressures for unnecessary specialisation in secondary schools. The use that is made of the machinery for planning, once it has been created, should be subject to the normal democratic processes by which governments are influenced. But unless the machinery for planning exists, the system of higher education can only become more chaotic, more expensive, and more wasteful of talent.

'We recommend that the grant for all higher education should be administered by a central planning committee in which the Secretary of State would have sufficient vote to enable him to implement a national policy for higher education. This Higher Education Grant Committee would be responsible for the central grant to each university and for an ear-marked higher education element in the rate support grant to local authorities. The national nature of the colleges of education and of the higher education element in colleges of further education is already recognised by local authority pooling arrangements. The present system of pooling local authority expenditure in higher education has a number of unsatisfactory features and a system of ear-marked grant supported by LEA expenditure in the case of LEA establishments of higher education and ear-marked grant supported by endowment or private funds in the case of universities would make possible a sufficient variety of establishments within which a national policy could be developed to provide a vital system of higher education.

'We are aware that such a system might be opposed on the grounds that it would constitute an unwarrantable interference with academic freedom. The legitimate freedom of individuals

and of institutions is a central and important issue in every society, but freedom results from a careful balance of the freedoms that all individuals and all the institutions that constitute a society would like to possess. It is not obtained by imposing no restriction upon the actions of one group of individuals at the expense of imposing unreasonable restrictions upon the actions of other groups. One aspect of academic

Dinnertime at a comprehensive school, Great Baddow in Chelmsford.

freedom is the need to secure that the economic resources that the nation devotes to the provision of education are used to the greatest advantage of the world community. Another is the need to avoid regimentation and the stifling of initiative in any part of the education system. It is necessary to strike a balance between the two and then to maintain that balance in the ever changing situations produced by a developing society. This can only be done if machinery is first created for striking that balance and the use to which the machinery is put is then subjected to the controls by which a democratic community resolves the clash of conflicting interests in all the aspects of human activity that impinge upon personal freedom. We believe that, as far as higher education is concerned, either the machinery for striking a balance does not exist or, if it does, its use is not apparent and it is therefore not being subjected to normal democratic control. Our proposals would ensure both the existence of the machinery and its proper democratic control'.

# Welfare in school

Following the 1944 Act the physical well-being of the children in the schools became very much the concern of the local authorities, which took over some of the responsibilities which had previously been carried by voluntary child welfare organisations. The schools' medical service kept a close watch on the health of school-children and was a valuable help in raising the general standards of child health during the post-war period. School meals and free milk played a part, too, in producing the most healthy generations of school children this country had ever seen.

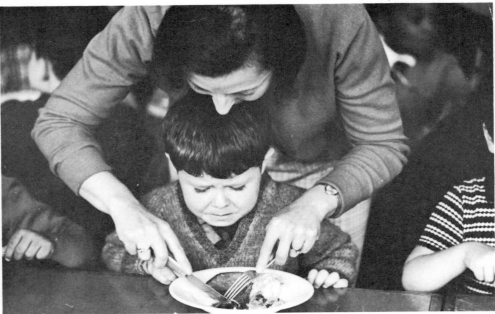

1. Another daily ritual, which still survives in the primary schools, was free school milk.

2. A bit of a struggle perhaps, but school meals are available in all schools for children of all ages as part of a subsidised service. Meals are free for children from the poorest homes.

3. Immediately after the war, during the period of food shortages, school dinner was often the most nourishing meal of the day for some children.

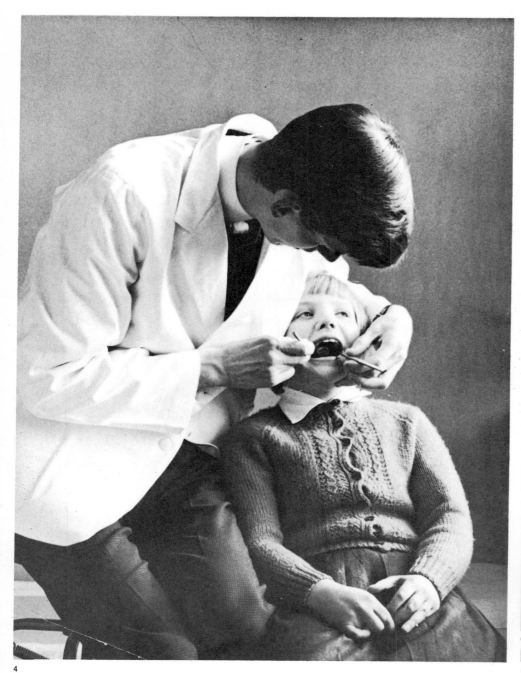

4

5

6

4. Not so popular, perhaps, is the school dental service which treats children free and also helps with valuable campaigns to try to improve dental hygiene in children's own homes.

5. An annual or biennial examination is not enough to ensure continuous good health and many schools now encourage health education classes and courses which can touch on any subject from dental decay to venereal disease.

6. Medical examinations for all school children keep a careful check on eye-sight and general health. Most defects discovered are minor but the school health service plays an important part in preventive medicine.

# After the war

Education suffered as much as any other part of national life from the ravages of six years of war. In 1945 the NUT put pressure on the government to demobilize teachers and students as quickly as possible so that a start could be made on increasing teacher numbers. Recruiting for the Emergency Training Scheme was actually done in the various theatres of war. As soon as hostilities were over a start had to be made on restoring and rebuilding the 5,000 schools damaged in air raids. With a shortage of buildings, a shortage of teachers, and inevitable confusion caused by evacuation, the education service was stretched to its limits, and to add to its problems there was an immediate rise in the post-war birth-rate. The 'Bulge' was imminent.

2    3

1. Appointed Minister for Economic Affairs in 1947, Sir Stafford Cripps has become a symbol of the post-war period of austerity and reconstruction. Economies hit education as much as anything else and protests were led by the NUT.

2. The pressure on space and resources led to many experiments to put roofs over heads. This is part of the first aluminium school – in Bristol – built by the Bristol Aeroplane Company (Housing) Ltd.

3. One of the 5,000 schools damaged by enemy action. This LCC school was hit in a daylight raid in 1943 and over 60 children were killed.

# Looking ahead

In spite of the post-war gloom, the Labour Minister of Education, Miss Ellen Wilkinson, herself a former teacher and 'scholarship girl', was determined to put the 1944 Act into effect. Against all the apparent odds she gave the go-ahead for the raising of the school leaving age to 15 as planned in April, 1947. 'A gesture of faith' the *Daily Herald* called it, and the NUT, welcoming the decision, called for an immediate increase in the supply of teachers to meet this new demand on the schools.

4

4. Ellen Wilkinson, though dogged by ill-health and accidents, led a determined struggle to create a new and better education service during the period of post-war austerity.

5. A question mark hung over these 'bulge' children in the primary schools in the late 1940s. Would there be enough teachers recruited in response to the vigorous drives launched by the government in 1947?

6. 1947 was the year of 'The battle of the school place gap', a campaign in which HORSA (the Hutting operation for the raising of the school leaving age) and SFORSA (the School Furniture Operation for the raising of the school leaving age) played a major part. As part of the programme for 14 year olds staying on these Norfolk girls visited Holt Hall for a special school leaving course.

5

6

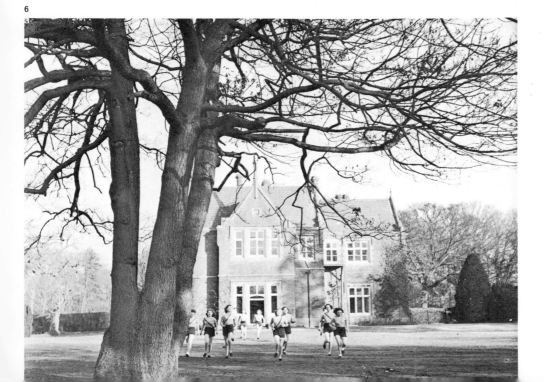

# After McNair

Hard on the heels of the Education Act came the McNair Report on teacher training which called for a drastic reorganisation of the profession and a significant increase in teachers' salaries. The committee estimated that the extra demands of the 1944 Act would require an extra 50,000 to 90,000 teachers and that the reorganised schools would eventually need 15,000 new teachers a year – double the number of entrants in 1938. The report proposed the setting up of a Central Training Council, and the organisation of the colleges on an area basis grouped around a university. It also suggested an extension of the training course from two to three years but this was rejected at that time because of the grave teacher shortage.

1. One immediate consequence of the McNair Report was the establishment of 20 Institutes of Education, almost all based on universities, to coordinate area training schemes. The institutes were responsible for courses, standards and examinations for college students.

2. To help meet the post-war crisis the Emergency Training Scheme recruited about 35,000 extra teachers, most of them in their 30s and 40s, and about two-thirds of them men. They were given a one year crash course, to be followed by two years of part-time study, and were taught in colleges improvised from army camps, orphanages, hutments and, as here at Trent Park, empty country mansions.

3. The National Advisory Council on the Supply, Recruitment and Training of Teachers was established in 1947 and a vigorous recruiting campaign followed. But supply barely kept pace with the increasing numbers of children in the schools and 1950 saw over half the children in maintained schools still in oversized classes.

2

1

3

# The expanding union

The membership of the NUT continued to rise and increased from almost 151,000 to over 184,000 in the ten years from 1940 to 1950. During the post-war years the Union played an increasing part as an educational adviser to the government, playing a leading role in the setting up of the National Foundation for Educational Research and reporting itself on nursery education, transfer at eleven plus, and the secondary curriculum. The post-war Burnham agreement introduced the 'basic scale' giving parity to teachers with the same qualifications teaching in different types of school. Yet battles over pay naturally continued and in 1949 a big new salaries campaign was launched for an extra £3 a week. The union also campaigned for higher grants for students on the Emergency Training Scheme, for new school buildings and for an expansion of university education.

4

5

6

4. Ronald Gould – elected general secretary of the NUT in 1947 on the resignation of Sir Frederick Mander. Now Sir Ronald, he was born in 1904, the son of a Labour MP. He was elected to the NUT Executive in 1936 and to the Vice Presidency in 1942.

5. The equal pay struggle continued throughout the 1940s. An average woman teacher's pay was just over four-fifths of a man's.

6. The first post-war conference to be held out of London by the NUT was in 1947 at Scarborough.

# The primary revolution

The 1950s saw the start of a major revolution in the primary schools. Stimulated by new research into the way children learn, this affected every aspect of teaching, from reading to the 'new mathematics'. It was based on the philosophy that children have a natural curiosity which can be harnessed to educational ends: they can learn, in fact, by discovery. Changes were to a large extent teacher inspired and supported by the NUT. All the major steps forward, already being taken in the best schools, were enthusiastically endorsed in 1967 by the Plowden Report, a major document on educational reform. The Report proposed the first change in the 1944 primary/secondary structure by favouring 'middle' schools for children from eight to 12 years old.

1. The Plowden Report called for 'positive discrimination' in favour of schools in over-crowded and socially deprived areas. The NUT had played a big part in highlighting the problems of 'slum schools' and the government responded to the public outcry with special grants for schools in educational priority areas.

2. The new primary teacher is less likely to be found standing in front of rows of children sitting at desks than advising individuals or small groups working on their own.

3. 'Parents must not cross this line'! The attitude was roundly condemned by the Plowden Report and closer home and school links encouraged. The NUT resisted attempts to take these links too far and allow parents to 'assist' and encroach on professional status.

1

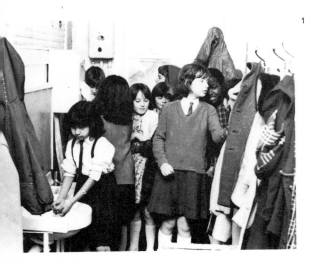

2   3

4. Changed methods of teaching were aided by a rapidly expanding technology of education. Radio had always provided schools broadcasts and in the 1950s schools television expanded rapidly. The 'telly' became a major influence at home and in school.

5. The child-centred approach to primary education was reflected in the new buildings which the NUT had fought for for so long. This school in Stoke Newington, East London, with bright sunny classrooms in which children can move around freely, was built as early as 1952.

6. By the late 1960s arithmetic by rote was becoming a thing of the past. This child is learning about weight by experiment.

# Fifteen to eighteen

The publication of the Crowther Report in 1959 was something of a turning point in the schools. The report looked critically at the education and training provided after the age of 15 and decided, in most cases, that it was just not good enough. To a large extent the report repeated the unfulfilled demands of the 1944 Act: it called for the raising of the school leaving age to 16, the introduction of county colleges, for more GCE courses in secondary modern schools and for an expansion of technical education. And to make this programme of reform and expansion possible it asked for another increase in the number of teachers to meet its new demands. Crowther was the first of the major reports which were to stimulate the programme of expansion and change which was already gaining momentum in the early fifties.

1

2

1. The Crowther Report endorsed the tradition of sixth form specialisation but made a plea for better use of 'minority time' to ensure that scientists were 'literate' and arts students 'numerate'.

2. Technical education, the Report said, has been neglected and should be expanded and improved to provide a coherent national scheme of practical education. Block release and sandwich courses should replace part-time study wherever possible.

3. Crowther also commented on the grave shortage of science and mathematics teachers and called for emergency measures to help solve the teacher shortage.

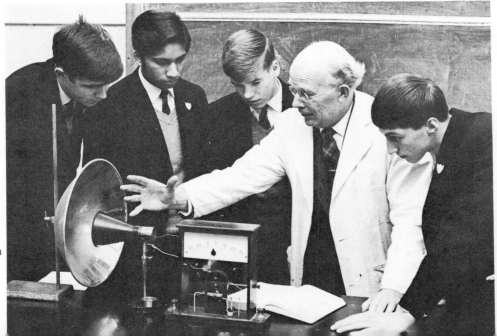

3

# Half our future

1963 saw the second major report on secondary education – the Newsom Report on children of 'average or less than average ability'. This called yet again for the raising of the school leaving age to 16, and this time the government responded by promising to raise it at last in 1970. The report considered in detail the education of the less able child who might well be reluctant to stay on at school, and called for a serious effort to overcome the problems of slum schools. As far as the syllabus was concerned, the report called for a range of courses related to occupational interests and paying attention to the personal and social development of the pupils. The places of religious and sex education in the curriculum should be rethought, the report suggested, and relationships with parents strengthened.

4

5

6

4. The Newsom report called for imaginative vocational courses for older pupils with increasing links with further education, the youth employment service and the adult world outside school.

5. The report also recommended more extra-curricular activities and suggested that schools might experiment with a lengthened school day for the 14 to 16 year old age group.

6. Many teachers seized on Newsom ideas and projects were started in secondary modern and comprehensive schools. Many of them involved 'Newsom' children in community activities with old people or with handicapped children.

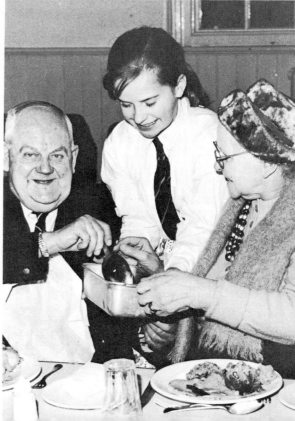

# The road ahead

There was progress throughout the 1950s towards a variety of educational goals, although as often as not the government and public opinion had to be prodded by the NUT by publications like 'This affects your child' – a 1953 pamphlet calling for improved school buildings. The number of children staying at school beyond the school leaving age increased throughout the fifties and in 1955 there were more qualified applicants for training college places than places available. But the teacher shortage was by no means over, and the chronic lack of science teachers in particular led to the introduction of special allowances – always opposed by the NUT – as an expedient to improve recruiting.

1

2

3

1. The new secondary schools were a far cry from the old elementary schools they were replacing: gymnasia, assembly halls and specialist facilities brought 'parity of esteem' in terms of buildings if not in public acclaim.

2. Technology came to the aid of teachers still too often overburdened by large classes. A teacher in a language laboratory can give immediate individual assistance to pupils learning a language orally.

3. Children's horizons widened with increasing affluence and school journeys to all parts of Western Europe became a feature of school holidays. Later educational cruises by liner were developed to carry large groups even further afield.

# A wider curriculum

A general broadening of the curriculum in both primary and secondary schools was often inspired by the enthusiasm of individual teachers. No holds were barred and experiments were carried out in every subject from judo to driving a car, in school hours and out. In some secondary modern schools particularly imaginative work was done with less able children who revealed too often unsuspected talents for artistic and practical subjects. Many became known for the outstandingly high quality of their creative work. Leisure-time and athletic pursuits were also developed as more schools gained access to playing fields and long lines of children assembling in drill order for formal PT became a sight of the past.

4

5

6

4. Golf, riding and athletics have all been adopted as sports in some maintained schools. This 13 year old at a South London Comprehensive school is being taught the rudiments of fencing.

5. Art education increasingly developed from drawing and painting and began to include pottery, sculpture and collage. These Hertfordshire teenagers have taken their massive sculpture out of doors.

6. Not every child can learn the violin but in some schools every child successfully mastered a recorder. This Kingston school certainly believes that every child can make some sort of music.

# The teacher's changing role

Spurred on by the major educational reports, and by research work, much of it NUT inspired, the role of the teacher underwent a subtle change during the 1950s and 1960s. In some secondary schools discipline became more informal, in others the teachers saw their role as more of a guide than a mentor to older teenage pupils. The influence of the Newsom report was especially strong, and its effects were not confined to teaching of less academic children. There was also an increasing emphasis in most schools on careers guidance, with a growing group of careers teachers spending the major part of their time on this work. Sex education became important too, as teachers realised that teenage pupils needed a more broadly based approach to emotional and sexual problems than a simple biology lesson could give. Some local authorities experimented with special counsellors to help adolescents with their problems.

1. Counselling parents has become a major part of many head teachers' work as children and parents have come to realise the major importance that education and qualifications will have in their lives.

2. An informal group of senior pupils at a London school discuss the problems – physical, emotional and moral – surrounding The Pill. The Plowden Report considered that even primary teachers should be ready to answer children's questions on sex.

3. The layout of many new schools led to a breakdown of traditional groupings for some lessons. Here senior pupils have a tutorial in a Coventry comprehensive school.

4. The General Certificate of Education replaced the School Certificate in 1953 and Advanced level soon became the key to higher education. It was followed by the CSE, which gave teachers a new freedom in designing their own courses.

1  2

# The examination explosion

The Crowther Report noted the trend in 1958: Robbins – in 1963 – produced a startling answer – and by the end of the 1960s successive governments had had to face an ever increasing pressure for provision of all types of education beyond the school leaving age. Even though the raising of the leaving age was constantly being put off – finally being promised for 1972 – voluntary staying on after 15 became steadily more popular. There were sharp disparities between numbers staying on in different parts of the country: while over half the 15 year olds in London and the South East were still at school only 30 per cent of the age group stayed on in the North East. These differences were naturally reflected in the numbers of examination, college and university entrants in the different regions but in spite of these discrepancies the trend was always and everywhere upwards. The pressure affected all sectors involved in educating the over 15s. In the schools the Certificate of Secondary Education was introduced in 1965 to offer secondary modern pupils another qualification at a lower standard than the General Certificate, and in the colleges, universities and in technical education there was relentless and increasing pressure for post-school places.

5. To meet the demands of increasing numbers of well qualified school leavers the Robbins Report recommended an unprecedented expansion of university education. Seven new universities were established, including this modern campus at Sussex, and the Colleges of Advanced Technology were given university status.

5

4

6

6. Crowther had called for a rapid expansion of all forms of further education. Robbins suggested the establishment of the National Council for Academic Awards to organise degree courses in technical colleges. In the late 1960s the more advanced technical institutions were designated as polytechnics and singled out for special development.

# The great comprehensive row

Even as the ink on the 1944 Education Act was drying and most authorities were introducing a tripartite system of secondary education, the London County Council was deciding to press ahead with a comprehensive scheme catering for all 11 to 18 year olds in similar schools. Comprehensive education was already part of Labour Party policy, and as early as 1943 the NUT conference resolved to support comprehensive experiments too. But progress after the war was very slow. In 1950 there were only 10 comprehensive schools in England and Wales; in 1958, 46, and in 1960 still only 130. The Labour government gave the necessary impetus to an already growing movement with the issue of the famous circular 10/65 which asked local authorities for plans to change to comprehensive secondary education. By 1967, there were 507 schools in existence and hundreds were being planned, although some authorities and groups of parents showed little enthusiasm for the change.

1

2   3

1. From the beginning there was opposition to comprehensive schools from some parents. These Bristol families, participants in a particularly fierce battle with the local authority, are marching to Hyde Park to protest.

2. Different local authorities found different solutions to the problems of reorganisation. Leicestershire pioneered a system of 'high' and 'upper' schools with a change of school at 14 for some children. Other authorities plumped for the 'middle' schools suggested by the Plowden report, and the West Riding of Yorkshire opened the first Sixth Form College, shown here, at Mexborough.

3. The LCC's first purpose built comprehensive school was Kidbrooke, completed in 1954. It housed 1700 girls and 90 teachers.

# 'Make teaching your career'

The unprecedented expansion in the numbers of teachers needed led to constant demands being made for the colleges to fit in more and yet more students. The colleges responded by allowing larger numbers of students to live in lodgings and by instituting some 'Box and Cox' courses whereby one group of students studied in college buildings while another was away on teaching practice, and vice versa. Special recruiting campaigns dominated the early 1960s to attract more mature recruits, especially to the technical colleges, and to persuade married women to return to their careers. Part time teachers were encouraged and nursery places made available for the children of teachers returning to the profession. The three year college course was at last instituted in 1960 and expansion of student numbers continued, with numbers rising from less than 16,000 a year in 1959 to nearly 39,000 a year in 1968. By the late 1960s both government and union officials showed some confidence that the end of the teacher shortage was in sight, although forecasts vary as to when it will ultimately arrive.

4  5

4. New buildings – here the City of Leicester College – and new attitudes marked teacher education in the 1960s. Many colleges became coeducational for the first time during the rapid expansion of student numbers.

5. Closed circuit television being used in a school so that a group of students can watch a lesson on number without disturbing the children.

6. For some students the Robbins Report proposal for a degree in education opened up the possibility of a fourth year's study leading to the examination for the Bachelor of Education degree. This was another step towards the NUT's ideal of an all-graduate profession.

6

# The changing face of the schools

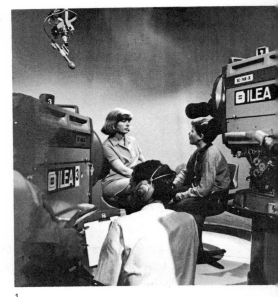

Where should we teach? What should we teach? How should we teach it? These are the questions which have increasingly occupied the profession for the last decade – a period which has seen an enormous increase in research and experiment in the schools. Almost the entire syllabus in the primary school has been subject to criticism and reform, and in 1964 the Schools Council for the Curriculum and Examinations was specifically set up to re-assess curricula, teaching methods and examinations. The Nuffield Foundation has also sponsored wide-ranging research projects in junior school language teaching and into the teaching of science and mathematics. Contributions have also come from the National Foundation for Educational Research, from the School Mathematics Project and from researchers into the teaching of reading: hardly an aspect of the school timetable has not been examined and where necessary rethought. For many teachers in secondary schools the impetus to rethink their subjects and teaching methods came from the experimental approach of the Certificate of Secondary Education which brought groups of teachers from different schools together to design their own courses.

1. A new dimension was added to lessons for many children by educational television. The Inner London Education Authority is one which has set up its own etv service and trains teachers to run it.

2. The initial teaching alphabet, developed by Sir James Pitman, is one of several experimental methods of teaching infants to read. Special texts have been printed in it, and it is found to help slow learners to read more easily.

3. Experiments with teaching machines, such as these in use in a Surrey school, give some idea of what the school of the future may be like.

4

4. Research into the design of primary schools led to the building of several experimental schools – including this one in North London – which were planned on the assumption that modern group teaching methods did not need small enclosed classrooms and that therefore spaces could be open-plan.

5. In some areas the teaching of immigrant children has posed a problem. Special language and reception classes have been started and specialist teachers trained to teach the immigrants English.

6. The increasing importance of mathematics and science in a technological age has led to major research efforts to improve their teaching in secondary and primary schools. Modern teaching methods indicate that quite young children can grasp mathematical concepts previously thought to be quite beyond them.

5

6

# Teachers' self help

Alongside the development of the National Union of Teachers, several satellite organisations have sprung up, which have been of the greatest significance to the profession, particularly in recent years. The Teachers' Benevolent and Orphanage Funds, The Teachers' Provident Society and the Schoolmaster Publishing Company were early on the scene. More recent times have seen the development of the Teachers' Assurance Company and the Teachers' Building Society. A brief history of these organisations is given here.

New Park, the Teachers' Benevolent Fund home for the aged.

## The Teachers' Benevolent Fund

The pioneers who founded the Union in 1870 soon realised that there would be a need for organisation to provide self-help and support for colleagues in distress. In the early seventies successive conferences discussed the formation of a benevolent fund and an orphanage and orphan fund.

A resolution to establish a benevolent fund was carried in 1875 and for an orphanage fund, in 1876. The funds actually came into being in 1877 and 1878 respectively.

The objects, laid down in the original draft scheme, were to give temporary relief to members fallen into distress or who had suffered accidents or incapacity, to grant temporary loans of up to £15, to make grants to widows and orphans and in special cases to grant annuities to old or incapacitated teachers.

The scheme envisaged that funds would be raised by subscriptions and donations from teachers and others, and from concerts, entertainments and other charity functions.

In the early years the growth of the fund was slow. The first balance sheet showed an income of £79 and relief and loans totalling £19.

The fund has grown enormously since then, and the Teachers' Benevolent Fund now has an annual income from all sources of £196,000. The fund maintains three homes for elderly teachers and a fourth is to be completed this year. It makes grants of more than £65,000 a year to children and adults in distress. About 3,000 applicants are dealt with a year.

The four homes are Wayside, Sunderland; Romaleyn, Paignton, South Devon; New Park, Stoke-on-Trent and Elstree, Herts., the new home. In addition the fund would like to set up a home in Wales. The fund also runs a housing association the first of whose projects was to build 41 self-contained flats at Birmingham for 60 people.

The development of the Benevolent Fund and the Orphanage and Orphan funds were completely separate in the early days, though the two funds shared administrative staff. They were combined in 1899 into the Benevolent and Orphanage Fund, and in 1967, the name was changed to the present Teachers' Benevolent Fund.

## The Teachers' Assurance

The Teachers' Assurance is the Union's own insurance organisation comprised of the Teachers' Provident Society and the Teachers' Assurance Company Ltd, commonly known as the T.P.S. and T.A.C.

The Union has always been very conscious of the personal welfare of its members and it was only eight years after the formation of the Union, that is in 1878, that the T.P.S. was registered as a Friendly Society to provide Union members with sickness and life assurance benefits on favourable terms.

As there have always been limitations to the benefits that can be offered by a Friendly Society, the Union and the T.P.S. decided in 1936 to form the T.A.C. which, as an insurance company, could offer to the membership an even wider range of insurance and house purchase facilities.

From 1936 until 1962 the T.P.S. and T.A.C. operated virtually independently of each other, but in 1962 it was felt that a merging of their operations would prove beneficial to the membership. Consequently, such a merger took place and, although the T.P.S. and T.A.C. still retain separate legal identities, the entire insurance organisation works under one Board of Management.

The Board of the Teachers' Assurance is comprised entirely of teacher members of the NUT and includes two members of the Union Executive to ensure close working between the two bodies. Thus the Teachers' Assurance is an organisation run by teachers for teachers. The management officials have however, had long experience in the world of insurance and are fully aware of the insurance problems and needs of the teaching profession.

The Teachers' Assurance thus offers a wide range of insurance facilities on attractive terms not only to members of the NUT and associated bodies, but also to the husbands, wives and children of such members.

The total invested funds of the organisation are now approximately £24,000,000.

The organisation has wide local representation in the form of one or more Local Secretaries in each NUT Association. Local Secretaries are teachers and members of the NUT and are only too anxious to be of service to their colleagues. In addition, there is a team of full time officials all fully experienced in insurance matters who assist the Local Secretaries in providing a personal insurance service to the membership.

## The Teachers' Building Society

There has always been a tremendous demand for mortgages for house purchase from Union members and it has always been very difficult for the T.P.S. and T.A.C. to meet this demand. In an endeavour to extend the facilities available for house purchase, the Teachers' Assurance, after consultations with the NUT Executive investigated the possibility of forming a building society.

Following these investigations, the Teachers' Building Society was launched in

December 1966 for the purpose of providing building society investment facilities and mortgages for Union members. The Society met with immediate success and during the first two years of its existence attracted investment funds of approximately £7,000,000 thus making a substantial sum available for mortgages for Union members.

Such growth however, proved to be too rapid, and in order to develop the Society on sound lines the Directors found it necessary to restrict the growth rate with effect from January 1969. Nevertheless, the total invested funds are now in excess of £7,500,000 and the Society is still able to assist members with house purchase although on a much more limited scale than in the first two years.

It will be seen that through its ancillary organisations, the NUT provides a wide range of insurance, investment and mortgage facilities for its membership and must be unique in union circles in having its own friendly society, its own insurance company and its own building society.

## The Schoolmaster Publishing Company

On December 19, 1871, the Educational Newspaper Company was founded, and in the following year the first issues of The Schoolmaster were published. The company, though independent, was associated closely with the Union, and the paper presented the Union's policy in forthright terms from the earliest years.

In 1909 the company was taken over by the Union and the Schoolmaster Publishing Company was formed with Executive members as the main shareholders. In January 1963 The Schoolmaster forsook its old magazine style of presentation, and under the new name of The Teacher was issued in tabloid newspaper form. In April 1967 the decision was taken to issue the paper to every school in Britain free of charge. The paper now prints more than 60,000 copies.

# Battles and victories

Whatever government was in power the NUT's battles for increased salaries and status seemed to continue without much respite throughout the 1950s and 1960s. In the early fifties pay negotiations were dominated by the demands of women teachers for equal pay. And – this battle won – 1961 saw a furious struggle against the economies introduced by the government in the throes of a financial crisis. But the Union had preoccupations apart from salaries. Between 1950 and 1952 it conducted a prolonged dispute with Durham County Council which was attempting to enforce a 'closed shop' on all its employees. NUT members finally handed in their resignations to Union officials in May 1952, supported by other teachers' unions and other professional associations involved. A strike in the autumn term seemed inevitable until an arbitration board decided in favour of the teachers and the County Council gave way. Less successful was a prolonged Union campaign in the middle fifties against the introduction of higher superannuation contributions for the teachers' pension scheme. On the educational front the Union waged a ceaseless publicity war to bring to the attention of the public the shortcomings of the educational system – the overcrowded classes and the slum buildings – which were contributing to a second class education for some children.

1. Oliver Whitfield, still a member of the NUT executive, played a leading part in the bitter dispute with the Durham County Council between 1950 and 1952. He is seen here (left) with Sir Ronald Gould, (right) and in the centre Mr. Charles Darvill, chairman of the Union's Law Committee.

2. Equal pay was finally granted in 1955. It was introduced in stages, bringing women teachers salaries up to parity with their male colleagues' by 1961.

3. The Burnham main committee in session with Sir Ronald Gould and NUT representatives facing the employers' panel. Salary negotiations continued to dominate Union affairs.

1

2

3

4

4. An attempt to cut the 1961 salary award by
£5 million caused a major dispute between the
Union and the government. This demonstration
outside Hamilton House made rank and file
views on Selwyn Lloyd, Chancellor of the
Exchequer at the time, quite clear.

5. A special delegate conference at Central
Hall, Westminster, voted on strike action
during the 1961 dispute.

6. Not all members of the NUT were always
happy with the way the Union was being led.
Rank and file reaction to national negotiations
was satirised by Giles in the Daily Express in
1961. 'However strongly we may feel about
Sir Ronald selling us down the river, Miss
Pummell . . . . .' reads the caption.

5

6

# Cut back

Economic crisis hit education again in the late 1960s and for the second time in twenty years it became difficult to find money for the new buildings and better facilities which the teachers had been pressing for. Local authority budgets were pegged and in some areas this even led to fears that some part-time teachers might lose their jobs and students coming out of the colleges might have difficulty in finding employment. The advertising campaign to encourage women to return to teaching when their children were old enough was quietly terminated and some mature entrants felt betrayed when fears of unemployment were publicly voiced for the first time since before the war. A particular disappointment was the deferment of the raising of the school leaving age – yet again – this time until 1972. There were also bitter complaints that the recommendations of the Plowden Report were not being implemented, although the government did make special grants to assist schools in deprived areas and to provide some extra nursery school places for children most desperately in need.

1. With a cut back on part-time staff by some local authorities making economies, the threat of unemployment seemed more real than for thirty years.

2. The 1944 Act proposed more nursery schools, the NUT has repeatedly called for them, and now parents are either involving themselves in 'do-it-yourself' playgroups or joining in protests like this one in London demanding more school places for the under-fives.

3

4

5

6

3. A question mark hangs over the 15 year olds who are still leaving school without any guarantee of further education almost thirty years after the Education Act recommended a leaving age of 16.

4. For students in a period of cutback and austerity there is the fear that there may not be jobs available when they are trained.

5. The legacy of the old schools, most recently condemned by the Plowden report, still remains a seemingly intractable problem. The surprise is merely that there is so much good education to be found behind grim, century-old school walls.

6. The overcrowded classroom is still with us with desks crammed together in buildings which went up over a century ago. In some schools teachers face almost overwhelming odds in their struggle to educate yet another generation of children in conditions which were condemned before the last war.

# 1970

So as it celebrated its centenary, the NUT was still in the vanguard of educational progress and still vigorously championing the cause of the children of England and Wales. It had come a long way since 1870. All but two of the Union's founders basic aims – adequate salaries and control of entrance to the profession – had been achieved; and the establishment of a Teachers' General Council, with control of entry, was at last under serious discussion. Now there were other aims to pursue. As the Union's prospectus described them, they included:—

The unity of all teachers (still apparently a long way off) and the establishment of an integrated system of education.

The establishment of a highly-qualified, publicly-recognised profession with emoluments and other conditions of service commensurate with the importance of the profession to the nation.

A four-year education and training course in Colleges of Education, under which the normal qualification for recognition as a teacher included a university degree, or the successful completion of a degree equivalent course.

Better conditions of tenure and service for all teachers, safeguards against unjust dismissal, and greater freedom for the teacher.

Salaries of teachers should be related to their qualifications, experience and responsibilities.

The basic objectives were twofold: to secure improvements in the education of the child and to achieve a higher status for the profession.

At the end of 1969, there were almost 300,000 members of the Union in nearly 700 local associations. There was a thriving Young Teacher movement. Apart from being considered as a major partner of the Department of Education and Science, and education authorities (although it was often in conflict with both), it was represented on more than 100 national bodies, as well as actively in the Schools Council, the CSE and GCE examining boards, the National Foundation for Educational Research, university Councils and Institutes of Education, and on many Ministry study groups. It had an unparalleled legal service for its members, the best Publicity department in the education service, sponsored several MPs in the Commons, and was the most respected educational union in the world, as well as the biggest in Europe. It operated the Schoolmaster Publishing Company and its weekly newspaper, *The Teacher*, the Teachers' Benevolent Fund, which was helping members or their relatives to the tune of £200,000 a year. The Teachers' Assurance, with funds of more than £24m, and the Teachers' Building Society.

The education service, in spite of the repeated cycle of Stop and Go, could also contemplate the centenary with satisfaction. Several gaps, of course, were still blatant. The NUT had exposed several of them in its proposals for the new Act. There were others that it overlooked. Thirty thousand students of university potential were still leaving school each year at 15. A surplus of teachers, even on the 40/30 class size limits, which were revoked in 1969, was not expected until 1978. The problems of the EPAs still remained largely untouched. Only about a quarter of all secondary school children were still in school at 16 (though the graph was rising steeply). Only about 15 per cent were going on to higher education. In spite of the NUT's declaration that all classes should have a maximum of 30 pupils, more than three million children were being taught in oversize classes. Young teachers were being paid a net salary of only £13 a week, and the basic scale still amounted only to £860 to £1,600, against the £1,000 to £2,000 which was the aim of the NUT, and which the Conference rightly described as 'modest'.

Yet the progress had still been enormous. British primary schools were the envy of the world. More and more students were being successful in the GCE and CSE, and it was estimated that by 1980, 170,000 sixth form students every year would be getting two GCE Advanced levels. Student numbers at universities and colleges had doubled in a decade to nearly 400,000 and it was confidently predicted that they would go up to at least 700,000 by 1980. A start at least had been made on helping the EPAs. Thirty new Polytechnics were being established. All but a few education authorities had implemented or prepared their plans for the switch to a national system of comprehensive schools. The eleven plus examination was on its way out, though slowly. The school building programme was reaching record levels, but still mostly just to put roofs over heads. The school-leaving age was being raised to 16 in 1972. Attention was at last being paid to nursery education. More and more pupils were staying on at school after 16. The Colleges of Education were being given more autonomy and it was expected that a quarter of their students would soon be staying on for a fourth year to sit the Bachelor of Education degree. Above all, there was an unprecedented public interest in education. All the national newspapers had accredited education correspondents, and a few even had two. And the budget for education had reached a new peak of more than £2,000m, or nearly six per cent of the gross national product, and was exceeding spending on defence for the first time in British history.

Another confident prediction, nevertheless, was that the budget would need to grow to

Looking hopefully to the future at Kingsmead Primary School, East London.

about £4,000m, and consume some eight per cent of the gap by 1980 simply to stay level with minimum demand; and on the eve of 1970 it looked as though the immediate preoccupation of the future was going to be the problem of reconciling the growing demand for education at all levels with a national income that was increasing only by about three per cent a year. The implications that would face any Government, Labour or Conservative, were outlined by Stuart Maclure, perhaps the most distinguished education writer of his generation, in his farewell editorial in *Education*, journal of the Association of Education Committees, before he left to take up the editorship of *The Times Educational Supplement*.

The more the education system grew, he argued, the more the pressure would grow to define the goals of the system, to decide what spending was for and to argue about the objectives to which this great engine of social change was directed. The education system had moved forward in the general direction of mass education, but the rate of development, and the proportion of money spent in the different sectors of education, had been determined not by planning but by organic growth. Yet now, if priorities meant anything, they meant ranking objectives in order, from which it was a short step to measuring the success of the system in terms of the objectives

and auditing its efficiency. To do this would mean finding a way, within the English ideal of distributed power, to translate general aims into specific curriculum goals, without lapsing into either despotic centralism or anarchy. The content of the new debate would be: The education system has already got a lot of resources. Now it should make up its mind about what it was trying to do, how to do it, and how much of it to pay from rates and taxes.

Another distinguished writer, Tyrrell Burgess, was also prophesying the new developments of the 1970s. The 1960s, he argued, had been the decade when pupils, teachers and parents came into their own to assert their rights as partners in education with politicians, administrators and 'experts'. They were also the era when higher education became a national issue, and Burgess prophesied that the eighteen plus, the Advanced level examination determining university and college entry, would eventually go the way of the eleven plus. At first, he suggested, teachers would show how ludicrous the selection procedures were and complain that the demands for university entry distorted the schools' curriculum. It would then be accepted that A-levels did not represent objective standards. After that, the anger of parents would make selection at 18 indefensible.

As the last chapter indicated, the NUT had anticipated the movement prophesied by Burgess, and it looked as though its main areas of attack at the start of its second

century were going to be the upper and lower ends of the system: higher education and nursery and primary education. Two areas still needed urgent attention, however. The Union had still to become the main pressure group and spokesman for secondary education. Secondly, it had to decide whether it was a professional association or a militant trade union. Yet with its membership of nearly 300,000 and the record of its first hundred years, it was undoubtedly the most powerful and influential educational organisation, outside Government, in the land. A summing up of its achievements is perhaps best left to Dr Asher Tropp, author of *The School Teachers*, who said in 1957:

'Without any of the advantages of the older professions, they have fought successfully for the welfare of the schools and for an increase in their status. They have shown how it is profitable to the State, the teachers and the children to enlarge the freedom of the teacher and to make educational administration a matter for joint consultation. They have proved that through the activity of professional associations it is possible to reconcile the desires of the individual to fulfil his professional conscience with the needs of the State'.

Asher Tropp left his last words to Sir George Kekewich, secretary of the Education Department of the Government in the late nineteenth century, who dedicated his autobiography to the NUT. It still remains difficult to quarrel with his assessment. 'They have always fearlessly attacked all absurdities

The campain for higher salaries goes on.
Young teachers demonstrate outside parliament in 1969.

of our education system', he said, 'have never cringed before officialism, have stood for progress, never for apathy or reaction, have constantly and consistently used their powerful influence for the good of the child, as well as of the teacher, and have been the mightiest lever of educational reform'.

# The new militancy

Teachers responded to the new era of austerity with an increased
militancy which led to constant clashes with the local authorities and the
government. Following a ballot of the membership the NUT launched
sanctions in selected areas during the 1967 salary dispute by withdrawing
its members from school meals duty, an area of long standing grievance
among teachers. Negotiations led to meals duty becoming voluntary
and in most areas 'lay' helpers were recruited to supervise school dining
halls during the lunch break. Dissatisfaction with salaries grew in the
era of wage restraint and the Prices and Incomes legislation and the 1969
conference in the Isle of Man was one of the most militant the Union
had seen for decades. It demanded substantial salary increases and by the
end of the year Burnham salary negotiations had broken down, thousands
of teachers had staged token strikes and the Union had called staff in
over 300 schools out on strike for two weeks – the NUT's first ever
national stoppage. The new decade looked set to start for the teachers
in a mood of exceptionally determined militancy.

1

2

1. The supervision of school meals during the
lunch break had become a focal point of teacher
unrest by the time it was used as a sanction in
the salary dispute of 1967.

2. A ballot on sanctions caused an immense
task for officials at Hamilton House who had to
count the votes and publish the results in the
summer of 1967.

3. The prolonged meetings of the Burnham
committee during 1967 were picketed by
teachers angry at the local authorities' pay offer.

3

4. The next big salary dispute was in 1969 when on one day in July a third of the schools in London were forced to close after thousands of teachers staged a half day strike to protest about low salaries.

5. The 1969 conference at the Isle of Man set the tone for a year of militant protests on the salaries front.

6. Overwhelmingly in favour. Birmingham teachers vote for further militant action in December 1969.

4

5

6

# Twenty-six years on

Twenty-six years after the passing of the 1944 Education Act some of the reforms that Act proposed are still not accomplished and question marks still hang over large sectors of the education service. We have, indeed, free secondary education for all, but the tripartite system and the eleven plus lie largely discredited while their replacement, a fully comprehensive system, is still in the throes of construction. The service has seen enormous expansion, so large in the field of teacher training that it is possible to foresee the end of the shortage of trained teachers without being laughed too much to scorn. But the legacy of the past still lies heavily in other fields, and especially in the primary schools which were left with the worst of the school buildings when the secondary schools were reorganised in the 1940s. Ramshackle buildings, antiquated plumbing and large classes still make the education of the deprived children in the ageing cities a sad and difficult business in spite of the devotion of their teachers. So teachers continue to agitate and not only for more pay but also for the capital expenditure which will make the schools fit places for the young minds which have their one chance of blossoming there. And one encouraging facet of the change which has taken place in the 26 years is that increasingly the teachers find that they are backed in their fight for a better education for all by the parents of the children they are fighting for. Education is more and more in the forefront of people's minds and like the teachers, people want more of it, and more of a better quality than ever before.

1. The 1944 Act wanted part-time education up to the age of 18 – this and the county colleges in which the students were to be taught are still a dream.

2. Another dream unrealised is for nursery schools for all the under-fives who want them. But this is a field in which parental pressure is growing and restrictions on building are being lifted to some extent in the areas of greatest need.

1

2

3. A question mark still hangs over the public schools, the subject of public and official debate for decades. The proposals for integration of the Fleming and Newsom reports still lie in abeyance.

4. Questions, too, surround the future of secondary schools as each local authority sets up its own version of a comprehensive scheme. Some seem determined to retain some form of selection but in any case the complete reorganisation of secondary education is a slow process unlikely to be completed much before the 1980s.

5. Another public debate centres around the future of the religious clauses in the 1944 Act. Is there any future for religious education in an increasingly non-church going society which now includes large non-Christian immigrant groups with many children in the schools?

6. For young teachers and students and tentative recruits to the profession this is a question still to be asked. Just how much are teachers worth?

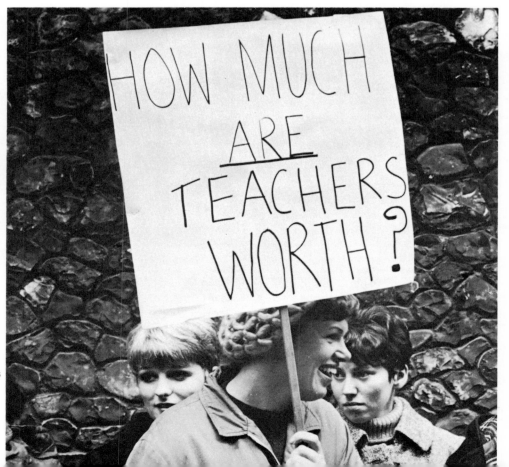

# Acknowledgements

Many officials and members of the National Union of Teachers have contributed greatly in the compiling of this book. They include the Union's Publicity Department, especially Mr Bob Shepherd and Miss Toni Griffiths, and the staff of the NUT Library, particularly Miss Margaret Shaw and Miss Janet Friedlander. Much initial research was carried out by Mr Ernest Naisbitt, formerly the Union's Organising Secretary. Sources of illustrations in Wales were investigated by Mr Cynan L. Humphreys, the NUT Regional Official for Wales, and Mr Dillwyn Lewis, of the NUT Glamorgan County Association.

The history of education in Bradford is currently being written up by a combined team of teachers and others in the education service, and the co-ordinating committee kindly gave us the benefit of much of their research.

The largest single source of illustrations is the Radio Times Hulton Library.

Other sources:

National Union of Teachers p.5 p.6 p.7 p.18 (3) p.46 p.69 p.73 (3) p. 77 (3) p.78 (2, 3 and 4) p.79 p.81 p.82 (3 and 4)
*The Schoolmaster* p.30 p.36 (1) p.37 (8) p.39 (1)
The Mansell Collection p.12 (2) p.13 (4 and 5) p.14 (1) p.16 (2) p.17 (6) p.18 (2) p.24 (1, 2 and 3) p.25 (4) p.44 (1) p.103 (4)
Cyril Bernard p.22 (2) p.33 (6) p.88 p.91 (4) p.96 p.97 (2) p.98 (1) p.102 (1) p.104 (1 and 2) p.105 (4 and 6) p.106 (2 and 3) p.107 (4, 5 and 6) p.108 p.109 p.111 (4 and 6) p.113 (6) p.114 (1) p.115 p.116 p.121 (3, 4, 5 and 6) p.122 p.124 (2 and 3) p.125 (5) p.126 (1 and 2) p.127 (4, 5 and 6)
Thomson Organisation (Topix) p.87 p.90 (1) p.91 (5) p.93 p.94 (2) p.98 (2) p.104 (3) p.112 (1) p.114 (3) p.118 (3) p.119 (4 and 5) p.120 (2) p.124 (1) p.127 (3)
Fox Photos p.70 p.73 (3) p.83 (6) p.85 (3 and 6) p.102 (2 and 3) p.113 (5)
*Children 1773–1890* History at Source Series by Robert Wood (Evans Brothers) p.36 (4)
City of Leicester Museum p.23 (5)
National Library for Wales p.43 (3)
Birmingham Post p.125 (6)
International News Photo p.101 (4)
London News Agency Photos Ltd. p.74 (1)
Mr J. E. Dunn, Deerhurst, Gloucester p.55 (3)
Castle Museum, York p.37 (5, 6 and 7)
Mr Dillwyn Lewis, p.42 (1) p.76 (5)
Department of Education and Science (Education Office for Wales) p.43 (2)
British Museum Newspaper Library p.49 (3)

Sport and General Press Agency Ltd. p.74 (2)
Keystone Press Agency Ltd. p.90 (3) p.100 (3) p.106 (1)
Carl Purcell p.94 (1)
Central Office of Information p.99 (5 and 6) p.110 (2 and 3) p.111 (5)
Richard Dykes p.99 (4)
Photomark Ltd. (Brighouse) p.112 (2)
Henry Grant p.113 (4)
The Press Association Ltd. p.114 (2) p.123
Newcastle Chronicle and Journal Ltd. p.118 (1)
Cartoon by Dickinson in *A Hundred of the Best* (Times Educational Supplement Cartoons) edited by Nicholas Tucker (Penguin) p.120 (1)
Daily Express p.119 (6)
Daily Telegraph p.125 (4)
Scarborough Publicity Department p.103 (6)
Bassano Ltd. p.74 (4)

*Local Education Authorities*
Oxfordshire County Council p.12 (1) p.35
East Riding County Council p.34 (2)
West Riding County Council p.41 (3)
Greater London Council p.47 p.49 (2) p.50 (1 and 2) p.51 (5) p.52 p.53
County Borough of Sunderland p.74 (3, 4 and 5) p.76 (1 and 2) p.78 (1) p.82 (1 and 2) p.83 (5)
County Borough of Great Yarmouth p.26 (4)
Derby County Council p.71 (3)
County Borough of Warrington p.68
County Borough of Bradford p.59 p.60 p.61 p.62 (1 and 2) p.50 (3) p.51 (4) p.57
Wiltshire County Council p.36 (3) p.49 (4)

*Colleges and Universities*
College of S. Mark and S. John p.21
Bishop Otter College, Chichester p.39 (3)
Borough Road Training College p.39 (4)
East Warwickshire College of Further Education p.71 (2)
University of Nottingham p.54
Elizabeth Gaskell College, Manchester p.55 (1)

Acknowledgements are gratefully recorded to the following authors:

Asher Tropp *The School Teachers* Heinemann
Brian Simon *Education and the Labour Movement 1870–1920* Lawrence and Wishart
J. Stuart Maclure *Educational Documents* Chapman and Hall
G. A. N. Lowndes *The Silent Social Revolution* (Oxford University Press)
W. H. G. Armytage *Four Hundred Years of English Education* (Cambridge University Press)
Olive Banks *Parity and Prestige in English Secondary Education* (Routledge)
S. J. Curtis and M. E. A. Boultwood *Introductory History of English Education since 1800* (University Tutorial Press)
Faculty of Education, University of Swansea *Pioneers of Welsh Education*
P. H. J. Godsden *How They Were Taught* (Blackwell)
Malcolm Seabourne and Sir Gyles Isham *A Victorian Schoolmaster* Northamptonshire Record Society
Malcolm Seaborne *Education* (Studio Vista)
P. W. Musgrave *Society and Education in England since 1800* (Education Paperbacks)
Gerald Bernbaum *Social Change and the Schools* (Routledge and Kegan Paul)
H. C. Dent *Education in Transition* (Kegan Paul)
H. C. Barnard *History of English Education* (University of London Press)
E. R. Hamilton *An Outline History of Borough Road College*
Tyrell Burgess *A Guide to English Schools* (Pelican)
Walter Roy *The Teachers' Union* (Schoolmaster Publishing Company)
W. O. Lester Smith *Education in Great Britain* (Oxford University Press)